COACHING THE JUVENTUS 3-5-2

Tactical Analysis and Sessions: Defending

WRITTEN BY
ATHANASIOS TERZIS

Soccer TeamTactics.com

PUBLISHED BY

SOCCER TUTOR .COM

COACHING THE JUVENTUS 3-5-2

Tactical Analysis and Sessions: Defending

First Published February 2016 by SoccerTutor.com

Info@soccertutor.com | www.SoccerTutor.com

UK: 0208 1234 007 | US: (305) 767 4443 | ROTW: +44 208 1234 007

ISBN: 978-1-910491-08-9

Author

Athanasios Terzis © 2016

Edited by

Alex Fitzgerald - SoccerTutor.com

Cover Design by

Alex Macrides, Think Out Of The Box Ltd.
Email: design@thinkootb.com Tel: +44 (0) 208 144 3550

Diagrams

Diagram designs by SoccerTutor.com. All the diagrams in this book have been created using SoccerTutor.com Tactics Manager Software available from www.SoccerTutor.com

Note: While every effort has been made to ensure the technical accuracy of the content of this book, neither the author nor publishers can accept any responsibility for any injury or loss sustained as a result of the use of this material.

MEET THE AUTHOR - ATHANASIOS TERZIS

- UEFA 'B' Coaching licence
- M.S.C. in coaching and conditioning

I played for several teams in the Greek professional leagues. At the age of 29 I stopped playing and focused on studying football coaching. I have been head coach of several semi-pro football teams in Greece and worked as a technical director in the Academies of DOXA Dramas (Greek football league, 2nd division).

I wrote and published two books "4-3-3 the application of the system" and "4-4-2 with diamond in midfield, the application of the system" in Greek language. I then decided to proceed in something more specific so coaches would have an idea of how top teams apply the same systems. I published further books with SoccerTutor.com Ltd which have become extremely successful and sold thousands worldwide:

1. *FC Barcelona: A Tactical Analysis*
2. *Jose Mourinho's Real Madrid: A Tactical Analysis*
3. *FC Barcelona Training Sessions - 160 Practices from 34 Tactical Situations*
4. *Jurgen Klopp's Attacking and Defending Tactics*

Analysing games tactically is a great love and strength of mine. I think teams have success only when they prepare well tactically. I have watched Juventus in many of their league and Champions league matches for the last few years and all of them during the 2013-2014 season. Over 1000 hours of research has enabled me to present a full tactical blueprint of Juventus and supporting training sessions in this book and the attacking book (other part of this book set).

Juventus are extremely solid during the defensive phase and the players read and evaluate the tactical situations very well. They tried to retain a numerical advantage at the back at all times which enabled them to defend aggressively against the opposition forwards in order to win possession immediately. If there wasn't a numerical advantage, they defended passively and played for time until a spare man recovered into an effective position. The midfielders also dropped back close to the defenders to help apply double marking of the forward in possession.

When pressing, the players tried to force the ball near the sidelines and two players would close down the player in possession. They would also tightly mark all the potential receivers as well as creating a numerical advantage around the ball.

When Juventus defended passively within the middle third they tried to block the through passes and retain a compact formation. If the opposition successfully made a through pass, the player who received between the lines was immediately put under double or triple marking.

Athanasios Terzis

CONTENTS

HOW THE TACTICAL ANALYSIS WAS PRODUCED FOR THIS BOOK

Athanasios Terzis has a great skill of analysing games tactically and watched every Juventus game in the 2013-14 season. This book is made up of over 1000 hours of extensive research and analysis of Antonio Conte's side.

The Steps of Research and Analysis

1. Terzis watched the games, observing Juventus' patterns of play and making notes.
2. Once the same phase of play occurred a number of times (at least 10) the tactics would be decoded and more detailed notes were written down, often separated according to the phases of the game and the various different tactical situations.
3. The positioning of each player on the pitch is studied in great detail, including their body shape.
4. Each individual movement with or without the ball was also recorded in detail.
5. Once all conceivable phases of play had been studied and analysed, SoccerTutor.com's Tactics Manager Software was used to create all of the diagrams in this book.
6. Finally, the key aspects of Juventus' tactics were assessed and are explained clearly with notes and detailed descriptions.

How the Tactical Analysis is Used to Create Full Training Sessions

1. Athanasios Terzis is a UEFA 'B' coach and has provided a full and extensive analysis of Antonio Conte's Juventus team, as explained above.
2. This analysis has been divided into specific tactical situations and has been used to create **40 practices** including:

   - Defensive Positioning of the Forwards to Block Passes
   - Defending an Open Ball Situation in a 4 Zone Positional Practice
   - Pressing Against a 3 Man Defence and Forcing the Ball Wide in a Zonal Practice
   - Pressing With the Front Block and Preventing the Switch of Play in a Dynamic 7 v 7 Game

3. Have you got the Attacking part of this Book Set?

   The full analysis and training sessions are included for the Attacking Phase, the Transition from Defence to Attack and the Transition from Attack to Defence.

HOW SUCCESSFUL HAVE JUVENTUS BEEN USING THE 3-5-2?

During the 2011-12 season, Juventus not only won the Italian Championship (Scudetto), but also managed to finish unbeaten with the best defensive record in the league. Juventus only conceded 20 goals in 38 matches (0.52 per match) and kept 21 clean sheets.

During the 2012-13 season, Juventus won the Scudetto and had the best defensive record again, only conceding 24 goals in 38 matches (0.63 per match) and keeping 19 clean sheets. During this two year period Juventus managed an incredible unbeaten run of 49 consecutive league games.

During the 2013-14 season, the team won their third consecutive Scudetto with an outstanding record of 102 points, conceding only 23 goals (0.60 per match). The manager Antonio Conte used mainly the 3-5-2 formation during these three seasons.

During the 2014-15 season Juventus appointed Massimiliano Allegri as their new manager. Allegri retained the 3-5-2 together with the 4-3-1-2 as his basic options for Juventus' formation. Juventus reached the Champions League final against Barcelona in this season.

Many think that the 3-5-2 is an old fashioned formation, but it has been very popular amongst Italian teams during recent years. The 3-5-2 formation was also used by many teams during the 2014 World Cup in Brazil. The application of the 3-5-2 formation by Juventus is said to be the most successful of this formation in modern football.

The purpose of this book set (including the attacking part) is to provide coaches with all the necessary information about how Juventus used the modern 3-5-2 formation in all four phases of the game. There is information about how to attack and how to defend against various formations based on Juve's tactics. This book set also shows in detail how the transition phases were carried out. Finally, the book contains many practices which can help coaches to train their players in order to apply the 3-5-2 formation successfully during all the phases of the game.

SEASON	2011-12	2012-13	2013-14	2014-15	Total
League Position	1st	1st	1st	1st	1st
Played	38	38	38	38	152
Won	23	27	33	26	109
Drawn	15	6	3	9	33
Lost	0	5	2	3	10
Win %	61%	71%	87%	68%	72%
Clean Sheets	20	19	22	19	80
Goals Scored	68 (1.79 pm)	71 (1.87 pm)	80 (2.11 pm)	72 (1.87 pm)	291 (1.91 pm)
Goals Conceded	20 (0.52 pm)	24 (0.63 pm)	23 (0.60 pm)	24 (0.63 pm)	91 (0.59 pm)
Goal Difference	+ 48	+ 47	+ 57	+ 48	+ 200

BASIC ELEMENTS DURING THE DEFENSIVE PHASE

The basic elements of the Juventus team during the defensive phase were:

- The good cohesion and communication between the three centre backs.

- Making sure to retain a numerical advantage at the back the majority of the time.

- The coaching between the players.

- The players informed their teammates about specific game/tactical situations and would guide them to ensure the appropriate reaction (coaching).

- The contribution of the midfielders would compensate when there was an equality in numbers at the back.

- Maintaining cohesion (short distances) between the midfield and defensive lines resulted in being able to double mark the opposition forwards.

- The attacking midfielders and/or the wing backs were key in situations when pressing against a four man defence.

There were also many more details about Juventus' defensive play that are fully analysed and presented in the following chapters.

JUVENTUS PLAYERS (3-5-2 FORMATION)

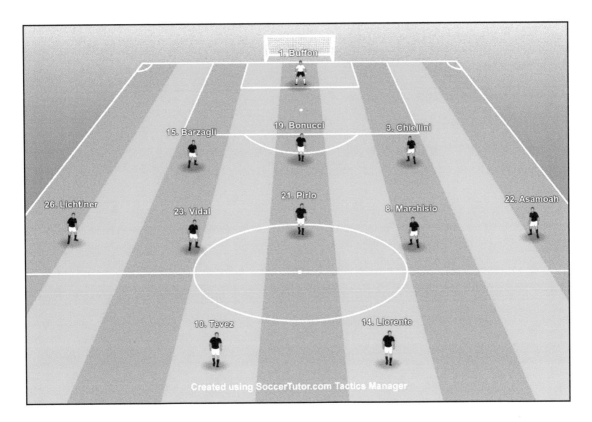

Goalkeeper: Buffon (1) is one of the top European goalkeepers of the last decade.

Centre Backs: The three centre backs Barzagli (15), Bonucci (19) and Chiellini (3) were very strong and capable defending in the air and on the ground. These three formed an extremely effective defence.

Wing Backs: The wing backs were full of energy and able to contribute in the defensive phase and the attacking phase. Lichtsteiner (26), Isla or Caceres on the right were more defensive minded. Asamoah (22), Giaccherini or De Ceglie who played on the left, were more attack minded.

Midfielders: Pirlo was the playmaker. He has great passing accuracy and dictated the rhythm of the games. Marchisio or Pogba played on the left. Vidal played on the right, taking over the role of the attacking midfielder (and scored many goals from 2011-2014). All of them were very flexible players with good contributions to the defensive and attacking phases.

Forwards: Matri, Del Piero, Borriello, Vucinic, Quagliarella, Tevez (10) and Llorente (14) played as forwards. They formed different partnerships, but all of them fitted perfectly into the system.

COACHING FORMAT

1. Tactical Situations and Analysis

2. Session for the Tactical Situation

   - Technical and Functional Unopposed Practices

   - Tactical Opposed Practices

   - Objective and Full Description

   - Restrictions, Progressions, Variations and Coaching Points (if applicable)

KEY

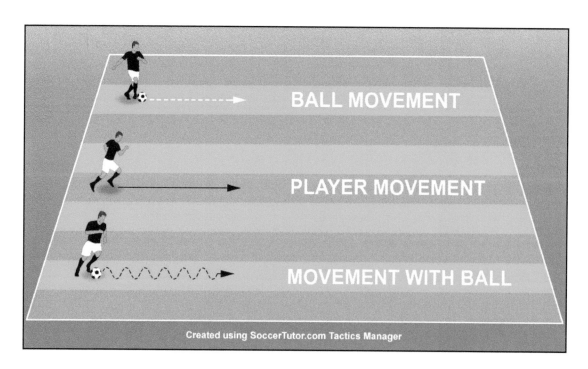

Created using SoccerTutor.com Tactics Manager

CHAPTER 1
THE 3 MAN DEFENCE

THE 3 MAN DEFENCE

The three defenders worked in collaboration. They followed the principles of zonal defending (pressure, cover and balance) and they tried to keep the appropriate shape according to the position of the ball.

The main aims were:

1. To maintain a numerical advantage at the back. The numerical advantage enabled them to apply aggressive marking against their opponents. If there was an inferiority or equality in numbers at the back, the defenders would not defend aggressively and would play for time instead.

2. To ensure that there was always a player who provided cover and another one who retained the defensive line's balance (according to the tactical situation).

DEFENDING AGAINST 1 FORWARD

Horizontal Shifts - Pressure, Cover and Balance

On the diagrams below there will be an analysis of the positions and the shifting (mainly horizontal) of the three defenders according to the ball position when they had one opposition forward to mark.

Positioning of the 3 Defenders Against 1 Forward Positioned On the Strong Side

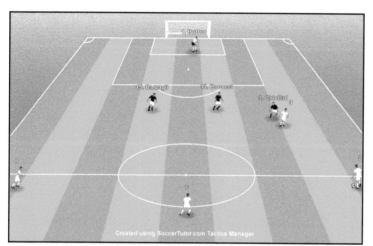

The opposition's right midfielder (7) has possession of the ball. Chiellini (3) takes up a goal-side position close to the white forward (9).

Bonucci (19) and Barzagli (15) are positioned in line with each other. Bonucci provides cover for Chiellini and Barzagli keeps the line balanced.

The numerical superiority is ensured as there is a 3 v 1 situation at the back for Juventus.

Closing Down the Receiver Aggressively On the Strong Side

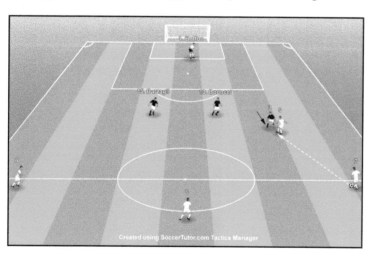

As soon as the ball is passed to the forward (9), Chiellini (3) moves to close him down aggressively, and tries to reach the ball first (if it is possible).

This reaction takes place as Bonucci provides cover and there is a numerical advantage for Juventus at the back.

Coaching the Juventus 3-5-2: Defending

Positioning of the 3 Defenders Against 1 Forward Positioned in the Centre

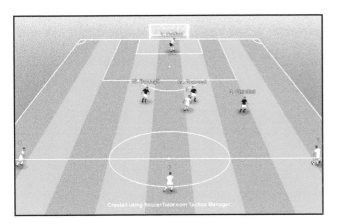

This time the opposition forward (9) is close to Bonucci. No.9's positioning forces Chiellini (3) to take up a position a few yards deeper and close to the other two defenders.

This positioning enables Chiellini to provide cover immediately if the ball is played to the No.9 in the centre.

Closing Down the Receiver Aggressively in the Centre

When the pass is directed to No.9, Bonucci (19) moves to contest him aggressively because Barzagli's (15) deep position enables him to provide cover immediately.

Chiellini (3) only has to drop a few yards back to provide cover. There is a numerical advantage (3 v 1) for Juventus at the back again.

The Left Centre Back Provides Cover in the Centre After a Pass in Behind

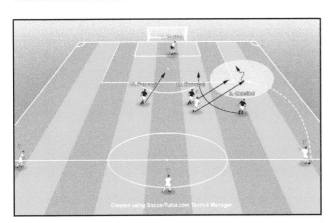

Chiellini's position close to the other two centre backs enables him to provide immediate cover for Bonucci, as shown in this diagram.

The opposition's right midfielder (7) plays a long pass into the space behind Chiellini.

Bonucci tracks the run of the No.9 and then Chiellini moves back into the space vacated by Bonucci to provide cover.

Recovering When Caught in the Wrong Positions

The three Juventus centre backs were not always in the correct positions. In tactical situations when the positioning was wrong, their reactions had to be different.

1 v 1 Situation in the Centre

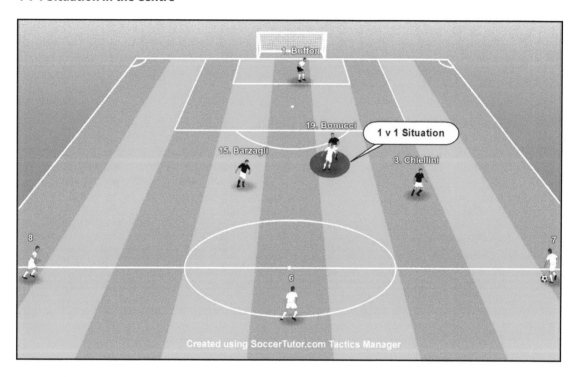

The forward (9) is close to Bonucci (19) and both Barzagli (15) and Chiellini (3) are positioned a few yards higher up the pitch than in the previous examples. The positioning of Barzagli and Chiellini prevents them from providing immediate cover for Bonucci. There is still a superiority in numbers (3 v 1) at the back but it can be turned into a 1 v 1 with a direct pass to No.9.

In this situation Bonucci would not be able to apply pressure on the new man in possession aggressively, but must defend in a more passive way. This gives his teammates time to recover and to reach an effective (covering) position. As soon as this takes place, Bonucci can then switch to apply more aggressive pressure.

 ASSESSMENT:

In situations when the forward was positioned on the weak side, the three defenders had enough time to readjust their positioning by taking advantage of the transmission phase (the time when the ball is travelling).

Positioning of the 3 Centre Backs When the Ball is in the Centre

In situations when the opposition player in possession was in the centre, the positioning of the three defenders was different and is shown below. The opposing forward could take up a position towards the sides or in the centre. If he took a position towards the side, the marking was usually aggressive as there was always a player ready to provide cover. In situations when the forward was positioned in the centre, the centre backs reacted according to the tactical situation.

If there was a player ready to provide cover, the forward was contested in an aggressive way. However, in situations when it would take a few seconds to provide cover, the centre back would have to apply pressure in a way to play for time rather than to win the duel.

Positioning of the Defenders When the Forward Was Positioned Towards One Side

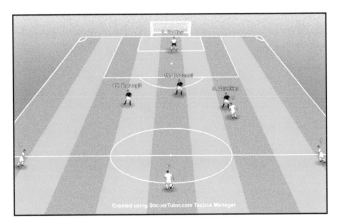

The ball is in the opposition's possession with the centre midfielder (No.6).

Chiellini (3) is in a goal-side position close to No.9 and Bonucci (19) is in a covering position. Barzagli (15) is a few yards further up the pitch because Bonucci has no direct opponent to mark.

Closing Down the Receiver Aggressively and Shifting to Provide Cover and Balance

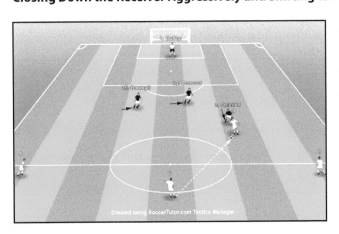

As soon as the ball is passed to the No.9, Chiellini moves to close him down immediately and aggressively while retaining a goal-side position.

The other two Juventus centre backs shift towards the left and retain the same formation which provides both cover to the first defender (Chiellini) and a numerical advantage at the back against the opposition.

Defending When the Opposition Forward is Positioned Centrally

Situation 1 - Closing Down the Forward Aggressively and Preventing Him from Turning (Correct Positioning of the Defenders)

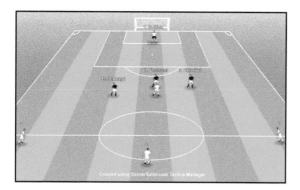

Bonucci (19) has a direct opponent to mark (No.9). That is why Chiellini (3) takes up a position in the same line with him ready to provide cover for a potential pass towards the white forward.

This positioning enables Bonucci to aggressively contest No.9 if the pass is directed to him.

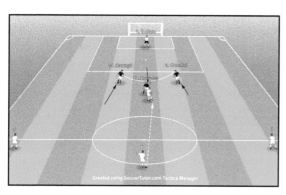

The ball is directed to the forward (9). Chiellini's position enables him to provide immediate cover for Bonucci who can aggressively contest No.9.

However, as Barzagli is unable to move immediately back to provide cover towards the right side of Bonucci, he ensures that the No.9 will not turn towards this side. That is why he moves to contest the opposition's forward (9) towards the side Barzagli is positioned.

Situation 2 - Incorrect Positioning Forces the Defender to Contest the Forward Passively

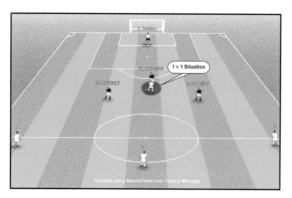

Bonucci has the forward as his direct opponent. However, in this specific situation neither Barzagli nor Chiellini take up positions which enable them to provide immediate cover.

If the forward receives and turns quickly with the ball towards the left or right beating Bonucci, the two Juventus defenders (Barzagli and Chiellini) would not be in a position to contest him. So Bonucci should contest the forward with the aim of playing for time so Chiellini and Barzagli can recover into effective defensive positions.

Vertical Shifts of the Defenders in an Open Ball Situation

In situations when the opponent with the ball was not under pressure and could pass the ball forward (open ball situation), the forwards would most likely make a run to receive in behind Juventus' defensive line.

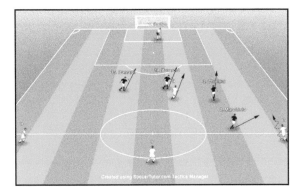

The right midfielder (7) is free of marking and also has plenty of space in front to move into. The 3 defenders move backwards for two reasons:

1. To cover the space in behind and track No.9's run to receive a pass.

2. To retain their shape.

3. To retain a safety distance between the defensive line and the man in possession, so the defenders have enough time to react to a potential pass.

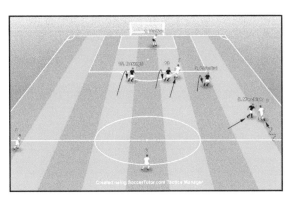

As soon as the midfielder Marchisio (8) closes the man in possession down and he is unable to pass forward anymore (closed ball situation), the defenders stop their backward movement and move a few yards forward with the aim of making the team compact again.

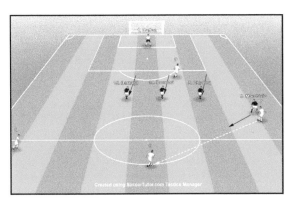

When the white midfielder (7) passes backwards, the defenders take advantage of the transmission phase (the time the ball takes to travel) and move quickly forwards together in the same line. This leaves the opposition's forward (9) in an offside position.

As soon as the ball reaches the feet of the new man in possession (6), the defenders stop and readjust their positioning.

Vertical Shifts of the Defenders When the Man in Possession is in the Centre

In situations when the man in possession was positioned in the centre of the pitch, there were two main elements that forced the defenders to drop back:

1. When the player in possession took advantage of the available space in front of him, the defenders dropped back in order to be compact and prevent through balls as well as give time to one of the midfielders to close down the man in possession.

2. When the man in possession was free of marking and an open ball situation was created, the opposition forwards usually made movements to receive in behind the Juventus defenders, so they dropped back to avoid a ball being played successfully in behind the defensive line.

Vertical Shifts of the Defenders Against a Midfielder Moving Forward With the Ball

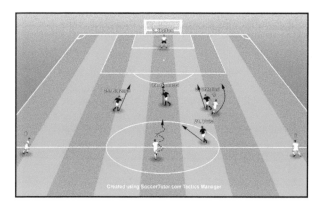

The man in possession (6) is positioned in the centre and has plenty of space to take advantage of before the defensive midfielder Pirlo (21) manages to close him down.

He faces the three Juventus defenders while the white forward (9) makes a run in behind to receive a through ball.

As the white midfielder moves forward, the Juventus defenders move towards their own goal to retain a safety distance and move inwards to prevent a potential through ball.

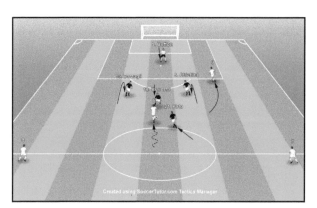

As Pirlo is unable to get close to the man in possession, he reaches shooting range, so the defender closest to him (Bonucci) moves forward to close him down.

At the same time the other two defenders stop their backward movement and step up a few yards to provide cover.

The goalkeeper (Buffon) gets ready to sweep up a potential through ball and the white No.9 is left offside.

Coaching the Juventus 3-5-2: Defending

Vertical Shifts of the Defenders During an Open Ball Situation

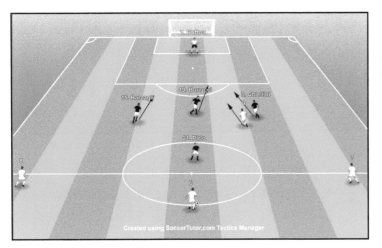

During a match there are also open ball situations when the man in possession does not move forward with the ball. In a situation like this the distance between the player in possession and the 3 defenders stays the same so they do not have to move back unless there is a movement from the forward/s into the space behind them.

In this situation the forward (9) makes a run to receive the forward pass in behind the defensive line. The 3 Juve defenders drop back to defend this kind of pass.

Example of When the Defenders Don't Drop Back Despite the Open Ball Situation

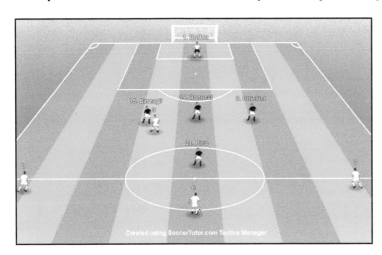

In situations when there was an open ball situation and the forward/s didn't make a move to receive behind the defensive line, the 3 Juventus centre backs stayed in the same positions, retaining their shape without dropping back at all.

SESSION FOR THIS TACTICAL SITUATION (4 Practices)

1. Horizontal Shifts of the Centre Backs (Pressure, Cover and Balance)

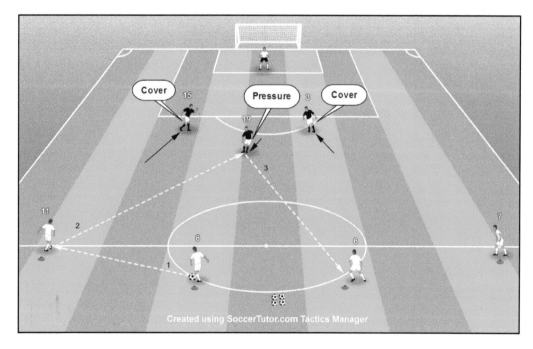

Objective

The three centre backs work on taking up the appropriate positions according to the position of the ball.

Description

The four white players are in positions indicated by the red cones and pass the ball to each other. The three centre backs shift (mainly horizontally) and take up positions according to the position of the ball (diagram 1).

Progression (Diagram 2)

As the practice progresses the white players (after passing to each other) direct the ball to the defenders. As soon as the ball is directed to one of the centre backs the other two should take up the appropriate positions as if this player had an opponent to contest - move inwards from their positions and back to provide cover.

The new player in possession (No.19 in the diagram) receives and after a couple of seconds passes back to one of the white players and the sequence starts again.

Coaching Points

1. The players use this practice to help them learn to provide cover as well as balance.
2. It is very important that there is a high level of cohesion between the three centre backs so they have synchronised movements.
3. The centre backs need to read the different tactical situations depending on where the pass is delivered.

PROGRESSION

2. Defending Against One Forward (Pressure, Cover and Balance)

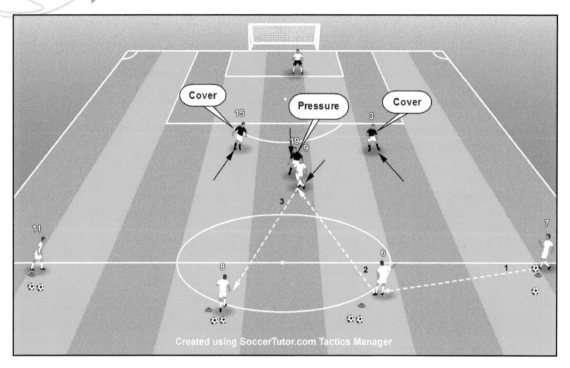

Created using SoccerTutor.com Tactics Manager

Objective

To take up the appropriate positions according to the position of the ball and to mark the opposition forward.

Description

This practice is a progression of the previous one so a white forward (No.9) is added. The 4 white midfielders are in positions indicated by the red cones and pass the ball to each other.

The 3 centre backs not only shift horizontally and take up positions according to the position of the ball but also have to mark the forward. As soon as the pass is made to the forward, the first defender (the defender who contests the forward) puts pressure on the ball while the other 2 provide cover according to the situation.

The forward (9) receives the pass, holds the ball for a couple of seconds, passes back to one of the white midfielders and moves again to receive the next potential pass. The white midfielders can also pass in behind the right or left centre back to test whether the defenders can provide immediate cover.

Coaching Point

The centre backs need to mark the forward according to his position, the position of the ball, the goal and the position of their teammates. Monitor this closely and use the analysis to see the correct reactions.

3. Cohesive Movements of the Centre Backs: When to Drop Back and When to Push Up

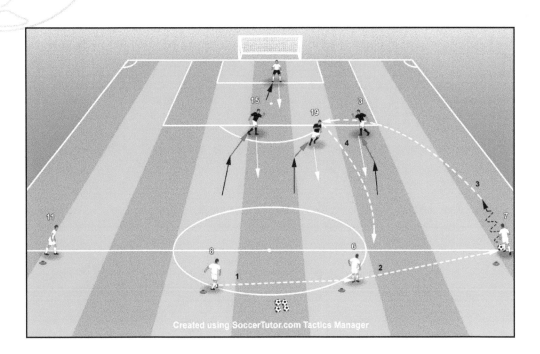

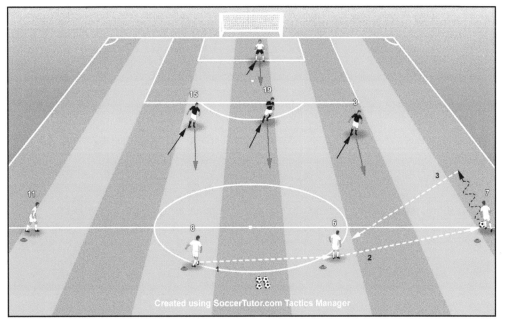

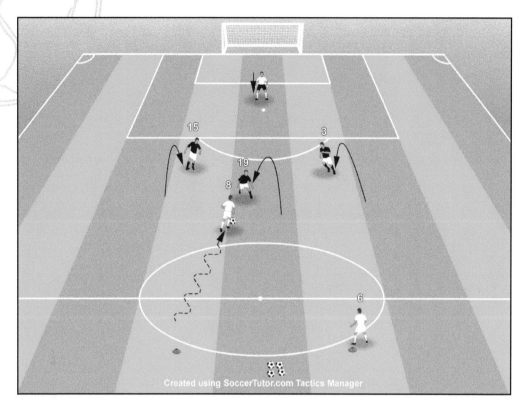

Created using SoccerTutor.com Tactics Manager

Objective

The players learn to read when there is an open or closed ball situation and then take the appropriate action.

Description

The 4 white players (opposition midfielders) are positioned on the red cones and pass the ball to each other. The 3 centre backs take up the appropriate positions and hold the right shape according to the ball position.

The whites are told to choose the right moment for one of them to move forward with the ball. They then test the defenders in 3 situations.

1. After running with the ball for 8-10 yards they can try a pass behind the defensive line (diagram 1).
2. After running with the ball for 8-10 yards they can stop and then pass back (diagram 2).
3. They can continue the forward run and search for a through pass (diagram 3).

The defenders should recognise the situation and take the appropriate action as a cohesive unit.

Progression: Add 1 and then 2 forwards for the white team who make runs in behind to receive and score.

Coaching Points

1. Players need to be able to read the tactical situation and synchronise their movements to remain compact.
2. The goalkeeper must also take part in this practice and move forwards and backwards with the centre backs.
3. There needs to be good communication and coaching between the defenders.

PROGRESSION

4. Defending an Open Ball Situation in a 4 Zone Positional Practice

Created using SoccerTutor.com Tactics Manager

Description

We play 5 v 6 (+GK) in 4 zones as shown in the diagram. The 3 black centre backs and the white forward (9) are positioned in the high zone (double the size of the penalty area). The defensive midfielder (6) is inside the blue zone. There are 4 white midfielders and 2 black attacking midfielders (22 and 8) in the low red zone.

The coach starts by passing to a white midfielder in the red zone. The aim for the whites (4 v 2 situation) is to create an open ball situation by receiving unmarked in the red zone or by running forwards with the ball (as shown in the diagram). The whites try to score and the black team have to defend the open ball situation.

The defenders have to react according to the tactical situation and use vertical shifts whenever necessary in order to prevent the forward from receiving passes in behind. As soon as he the ball leaves the red zone, the defensive midfielder (21) closes down the man in possession. The white player can pass back to his teammates in the red zone which creates a closed ball situation, and the black defenders should then move forwards together.

Only one white player (the man in possession) can move out of the red low zone and the two black attacking midfielders (8 and 22) must stay within the red zone throughout.

Progression: Add an extra white forward in the high zone to create a 3 v 2 situation instead of 3 v 1.

DEFENDING AGAINST 2 FORWARDS

DEFENDING AGAINST 2 FORWARDS

When Juventus had to deal with two forwards, the defenders took up the correct positioning in order to both mark the forwards and cover the space. They could contest the player in possession aggressively or in a more passive way (playing for time) depending on the tactical situation.

The centre backs could follow the forwards' movements to drop off deeper if the tactical situation favoured this reaction. In any other situation, they preferred to let the forwards drop off without following them. Whether to follow the forwards or not often depended on other factors, such as the positioning of the wing backs and the distance between the midfielders and the defenders (compactness of the rear block). The two last factors will be analysed in a later chapter. On the following diagrams there will be an analysis of the positioning of the defenders according to the various positions of the forwards.

Contesting the Forward in Possession Aggressively

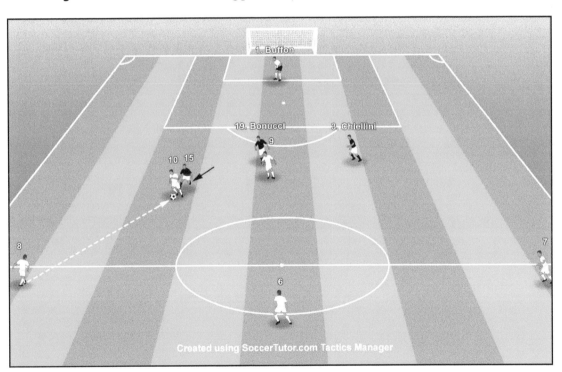

In this situation the 3 Juventus centre backs have to deal with 2 forwards. The ball is with the left midfielder (8) and the 3 Juventus defenders take up positions which ensure balance, cover and a numerical advantage.

Barzagli (15) marks No.10, Bonucci (19) marks No.9 and also provides cover to Barzagli. Chiellini (3) keeps the line balanced. As soon as the ball is passed to No.10, Barzagli moves to contest him aggressively. Bonucci provides cover and there is a numerical advantage at the back for Juventus.

Following the Forward's Movement at the Wrong Time

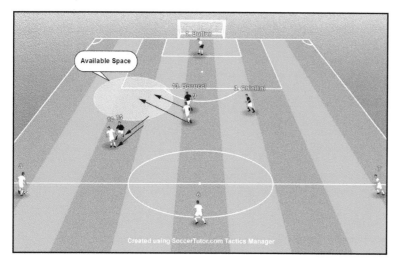

In this situation, the white No.10 drops into a deeper position and Barzagli (15) follows him, so space is created on the right side of the Juventus defence.

This available space can be attacked by the opposition's forward (9) and Barzagli will be too far away to provide cover for Bonucci (19).

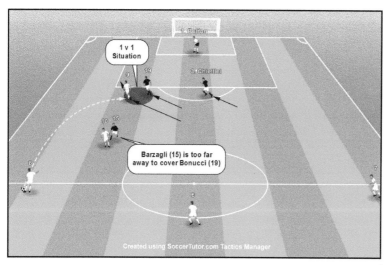

The pass is played behind Barzagli and towards the created space. Bonucci (19) has to defend against No.9 (1 v 1). Barzagli (15) is too far away to move into a covering position.

One option is the extensive shift of Chiellini towards the side, but this reaction may unbalance the line and leave a gap in the centre of defence. The appropriate reaction in this situation is for Barzagli not to follow the movement and leave No.10 under a midfielder's supervision, staying close to the other 2 centre backs. This is so that when a situation occurs like this and there is a forward pass, he will be close to Bonucci and ready to provide cover.

This keeps the line balanced as Chiellini will avoid the extensive shift. For a proper reaction like this there needs to be good communication (coaching) between the centre backs who will inform Barzagli to stay close to them.

Coaching the Juventus 3-5-2: Defending

Effective Defending Against 2 Forwards (Correct Positioning)

The Correct Positioning Enables Aggressive Defending With the Forward in Possession

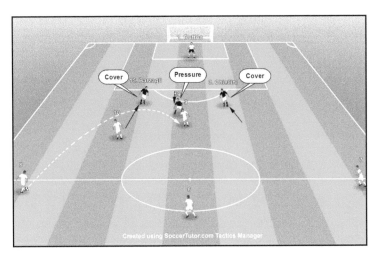

The right centre back on the strong side (Barzagli - No.15) stays deep close to his teammates. This kind of positioning is effective against the positioning of the opposing forwards shown in the diagram.

If the pass is directed to the white forward (9), Bonucci (19) can aggressively contest him, as both Chiellini (3) and especially Barzagli are able to provide immediate cover.

Allowing the Forward to Drop Deep Without Marking

If the forward (9) drops deeper to provide a potential passing option to the man in possession, Bonucci (19) wouldn't follow him because that would leave Barzagli (15) without cover and leave a gap in the centre of defence.

Bonucci either passes the responsibility of No.9's marking to one of the midfielders or puts him under pressure after the pass is made towards him (taking advantage of the transmission phase - the time the ball takes to travel).

Coaching the Juventus 3-5-2: Defending

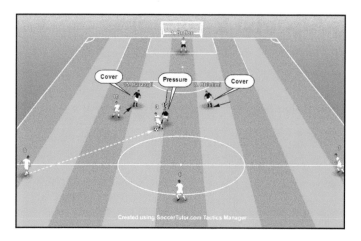

As soon as the pass is made from No.8 to No.9, Bonucci takes advantage of the transmission phase and moves forward to put pressure on the new man in possession.

The other two defenders provide cover. Juventus are able to deal with the situation successfully and are not left unbalanced by the opposition forward's movement.

How the Wrong Positioning Can Cause Problems When the Forward Drops Deep

If Bonucci (19) follows the forward's (his direct opponent No.9) movement before the pass towards him is made, the man in possession (8) can direct the ball to No.10. The No.10 would then be able to attack Barzagli in a 1 v 1 situation, as Bonucci is unable to provide cover.

Additionally if Chiellini (3) makes an extensive shift towards the right to provide cover to Barzagli (15), the defensive line's balance will be lost.

Tracking the Forward Dropping Deep Without Causing Problems

In this situation the No.10 drops deep to provide a potential passing option to the man in possession, while the forward (9) is positioned on the weak side (away from exploiting the space).

As Bonucci is in a covering position and there is no opponent who can take advantage of the created space on Juventus' right side, Barzagli is coached to follow his marker.

Communication is essential for good collaboration. There is a numerical advantage at the back for Juventus.

The Correct Defensive Positioning When Both Forwards are Positioned On the Weak Side

The Right Centre Back On the Strong Side Stays Close to His Teammates

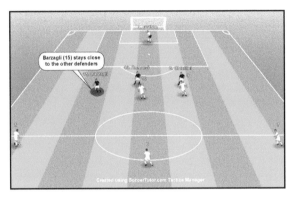

Both Bonucci (19) and Chiellini (3) have direct opponents to mark in this situation and they take up goal-side positions.

Barzagli (15) has no player to mark, but he reads the tactical situation (or he is coached) and stays close to the other 2 centre backs in order to provide cover if necessary, as well as maintain a numerical advantage for Juventus at the back.

Maintaining a Numerical Advantage and Providing Cover (1)

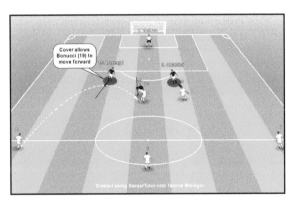

The pass is directed to the forward (10).

As Chiellini is able to provide cover to Bonucci (19) immediately and Barzagli is not far away from being the extra man for Juventus, Bonucci moves to aggressively contest No.10.

Maintaining a Numerical Advantage and Providing Cover (2)

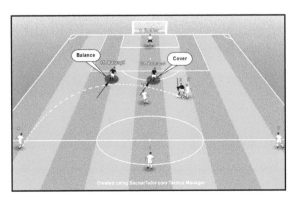

The pass is directed to No.9 this time. Chiellini moves to contest the new ball carrier aggressively as Bonucci moves into a covering position.

Barzagli is in a balanced position which enables him to ensure that Juventus outnumber the opposition at the back.

Defending When the Ball is in the Centre and the Forwards are Near the Sidelines

The Correct Defensive Positioning When the Ball is in the Centre

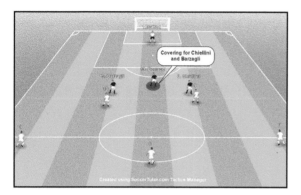

The opposition's centre midfielder has possession. The 3 Juventus centre backs take up the correct positions.

Bonucci (19) is in a covering position to both Barzagli (15) and Chiellini who are goal-side of their direct opponents.

Maintaining a Numerical Advantage and Providing Cover

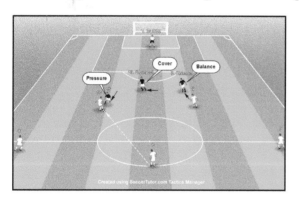

The pass is directed to white No.10 and Barzagli (15) contests him aggressively as there is already a player behind him (Bonucci) who provides cover.

There is also as an extra player for Juventus to maintain a numerical advantage at the back (3 v 2 situation).

Tracking the Forward Dropping Deep

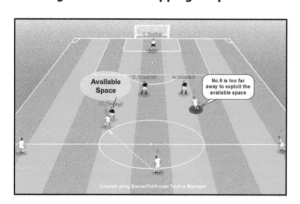

If the No.10 drops off, Barzagli can follow his movement. This is because there is no player to exploit the space created behind Barzagli.

This defensive reaction can only take place through the continuous communication (coaching) between the players.

One Forward in the Centre and the Other One Wide - The Wrong Reaction

Barzagli (15) decides to follow No.10's movement, so space is created behind him. The white No.9 can take advantage of this space in a 1 v 1 situation against Bonucci (19).

A better reaction would be for Barzagli to pass the responsibility of No.10's marking to one of the midfielders and stay close to the other centre backs. He would then be able to provide immediate cover to Bonucci if a through pass was made.

One Forward in the Centre and the Other One Wide - The Right Reaction

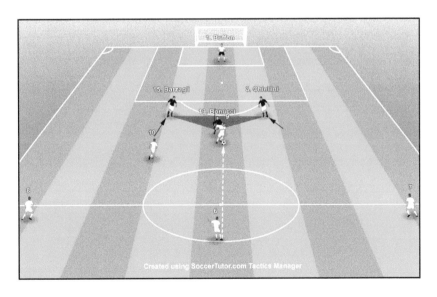

If Barzagli is in a position which enables him to drop back and provide cover very quickly, then as soon as the pass is directed to No.9, Bonucci is able to contest the new man in possession aggressively.

Bonucci moves to close down No.9 and prevent him from turning towards Juventus' right side because Barzagli is in an advanced position.

Barzagli then has time to drop back into a covering position and forms a defensive triangle behind Bonucci with Chiellini.

Incorrect Positioning of the Left and Right Centre Backs When the Ball is in the Centre

Advanced Positioning of the Left and Right Centre Backs

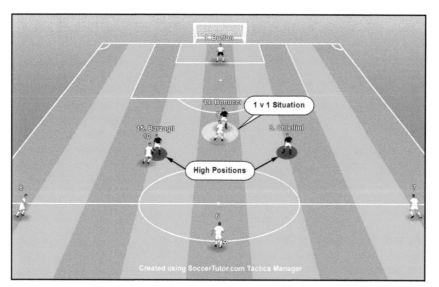

In this tactical situation both Chiellini (3) and Barzagli (15) are in advanced positions.

This positioning does not enable the left or right centre back to provide immediate cover to Bonucci (19) who has a player to mark (No.9) in a 1 v 1 situation.

Playing for Time for Teammates to Provide Cover

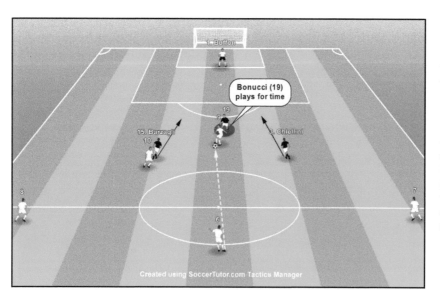

As soon as the ball is directed to No.9, Bonucci has to play for time and the other two centre backs move back into covering positions behind him.

As soon as Barzagli and Chiellini get back into covering positions, Bonucci can then switch to a more aggressive way of defending.

Recovering from Bad Defensive Positioning Using Offside Tactics

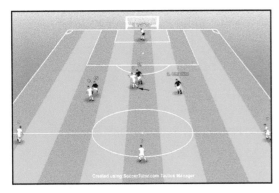

This diagram shows how offside tactics can be used to make up for bad defensive positioning. Chiellini (3) is in a more advanced position than Bonucci (19). If the ball is passed to No.9, Bonucci (19) will not be able to aggressively contest him - this is because Chiellini is too far away to provide immediate cover.

However, as shown in the next two diagrams, the offside trap can easily be used to prevent the opposition from taking advantage of the potential 1 v 1 situation.

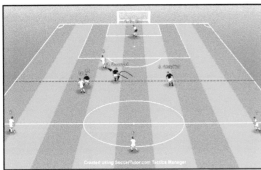

Bonucci (19) follows No.9's movement behind Barzagli (15) and as soon as he realises that the ball cannot be passed forward, he steps up and leaves the centre forward (9) in an offside position.

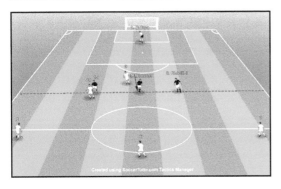

In this situation No.9 is not moving forward but he is focused on the ball carrier. Bonucci steps up a few yards to be in line with Chiellini (3) and leaves No.9 in an offside position again.

ASSESSMENT:

The centre back must find the right moment to step up - this can be when the ball carrier kicks the ball away from their feet or they are unable to pass it forward immediately because their head is down. If the player in possession is ready to pass the ball forward, stepping forward for the defender can be a very risky move. Another important element is the communication between Chiellini (3) and Bonucci (19) - Chiellini needs to be aware of the situation and not drop deeper, preventing him from playing the forward onside.

Coaching the Juventus 3-5-2: Defending

SESSION FOR THIS TACTICAL SITUATION (4 Practices)

1. Recovering from Bad Defensive Positioning Using Offside Tactics

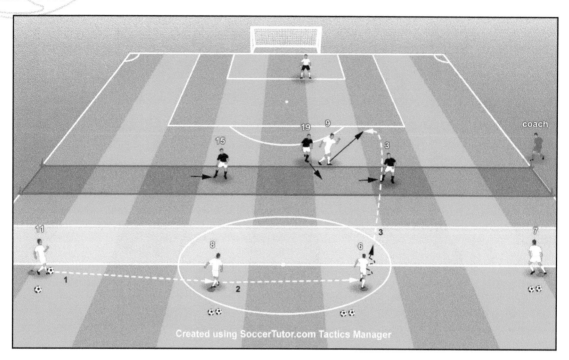

Description

Using half a full sized pitch we mark out a zone (blue) where the right and left centre backs are positioned, as shown in the diagram. The middle centre back (19) and the opposition forward (9) are positioned outside the blue zone. There is also a white zone near the halfway line where the white midfielders (positioned on the red cones) must pass towards their forward from.

The 4 white midfielders pass the ball to each other and the 3 black centre backs shift together in relation to the position of the ball. No.19 marks the white forward.

Once one of the midfielders enters the white zone with the ball, the white forward (9) is ready to receive either a pass to feet (outside the blue zone) or a pass into the space in behind. The centre back (19) steps forwards into the blue zone to leave the forward in an offside position. If he feels that his timing is not right to leave the opponent offside he should decide to follow his run. The coach is in a position to judge the defender's decision.

Coaching Points

1. As the middle centre back (19) is in a deeper position than the other 2 centre backs this practice is focussed around his judgment and decision making.

2. Reading the tactical situation and making the right choice at the right moment is the key to this practice.

Coaching the Juventus 3-5-2: Defending

2. Defending Against 2 Opposition Forwards by Applying Pressure, Providing Cover and Maintaining Balance

Created using SoccerTutor.com Tactics Manager

Objective

To practice moving collectively in relation to the position of the ball and marking 2 forwards.

Description

The 4 white midfielders are positioned by the red cones and pass the ball to each other until one of them passes to one of the forwards (No.6 in diagram). The 3 centre backs shift together in relation to the position of the ball and mark the 2 forwards. The forwards and centre backs mainly shift horizontally.

The first defender (the defender who contests the forward who receives) puts pressure on the ball while the other 2 provide cover and balance according to the situation. The forward who receives holds the ball for a couple of seconds, passes back to one of the white midfielders and moves together with his teammate to receive again. The white midfielders can also pass in behind the left or right centre back for a forward to run onto. This tests the defenders' reactions as they must immediately provide cover.

Coaching Points

1. Defenders must take up the appropriate positions according to the ball position and mark their opponents.

2. Players learn to provide cover and balance, using synchronised movements (reading the tactical situation).

PROGRESSION

3. Judging the Right Time to Track Forwards Dropping Deep When the Defence is Balanced

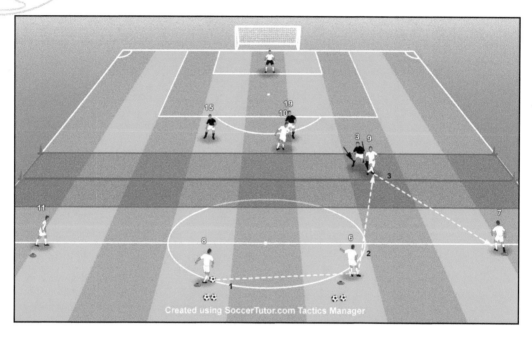

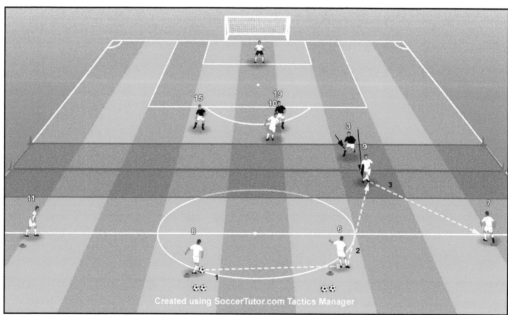

Objective

To practice the right moment to follow the opposition forwards when they drop deep in situations when the 3 centre backs have good positioning.

Description

This practice is a progression of the previous one and the defenders again take up the appropriate positions according to the position of the ball and mark the 2 white forwards (No.9 and No.10).

The aim of this practice is to create situations in which the centre backs have to decide whether or not to track the forwards when they drop deep to receive.

We mark out two zones as shown (10 yards x the width of the pitch), one blue and one red. The 4 white midfielders are positioned by the red cones and pass the ball to each other. The 3 centre backs and the white forwards start positioned outside the zones and move constantly.

The defenders follow the forwards when they drop into the blue zone to receive, but if they move into the red zone they have to decide whether to follow or not according to the situation (as shown in the 2 diagrams).

The forward who receives holds the ball for a couple of seconds, passes back to one of the white players and the defender and forward move outside of the zones to start again.

Coaching Points

1. The defenders (mainly the central one) should use short key words - 'STAY' when the defender should not follow the forward's movement or 'GO' when he should.
2. The timing of the defender's movement is key as it must be precisely at the right moment.
3. The forwards should check away from their marker before moving to receive in the zones.

VARIATION

4. Judging the Right Time to Track Forwards Dropping Deep When the Defence is Imbalanced

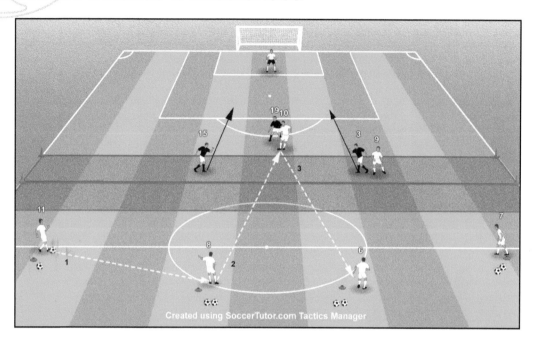

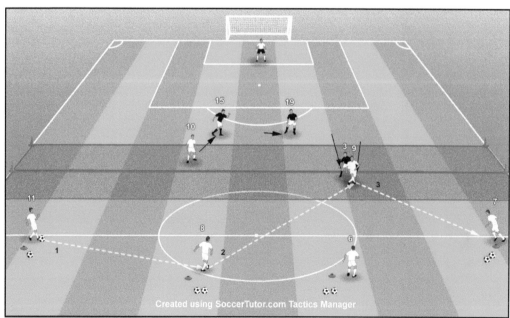

Objective

To practice the right moment to follow the opposition forwards when they drop deep in situations when the left and right centre backs are in the wrong positions (too advanced).

Description

This is a variation of the previous practice. During a match there are situations where the defenders are in the wrong positions. The aim of this practice is to coach the correct response when they are faced with this tactical problem.

This time the right and left centre backs and the white forward (9) are positioned inside the blue zone. The other centre back (19) is positioned behind and outside of the zones. The white No.10 is free to move anywhere. The right and left centre backs (No.15 and No.3) are not allowed to move outside of the blue zone until there is a pass towards a white forward.

The forwards have the freedom to receive either in an advanced area (the blue zone) or drop even deeper to receive inside the red zone when they feel it's the right time to do so. They receive, hold the ball for a couple of seconds, pass back to one of the white players and then move to try and receive again.

The defenders coach each other and must make the correct decisions:

- **Diagram 1:** No.10 receives in a central position outside the zones, so the left and right centre backs (No.15 and No.3) both drop back to provide cover for No.19.

- **Diagram 2:** The pass is wider and the No.9 drops deep to receive. The situation favours the left centre back (3) contesting the new ball carrier aggressively. No.19 shifts across to provide cover and No.15 drops back to provide balance.

Coaching Points

1. The defenders have to learn when to use aggressive marking and when to play for time, all in relation to the tactical situation.
2. The defenders must use synchronised movements to provide cover and balance.

DEFENDING AGAINST 3 FORWARDS

Defending Against 3 Narrow Forwards: Ball Near the Sideline (Wing Back in Effective Position)

When Juventus had to face a team that played with 3 narrow forwards (e.g. using the 3-4-3 formation), in order for the team to maintain their numerical advantage at the back, one of the two wing backs (usually the one on the weak side) had to drop back and form a 4 man defence.

In order for this player to be effective, he had to position himself towards the centre and behind the line of where the opposition's weak side forward was.

Effective Positioning of the Wing Back On the Weak Side When the Ball is Near the Sideline

In this situation Juventus' 3 man defence has to deal with 3 opposition forwards (11, 9 and 7).

The left wing back Asamoah (22) puts pressure on the player in possession while Chiellini (3) is marking No.7 (goal-side) and provides cover for Asamoah. Barzagli (15) and Bonucci (19) are positioned in line with each other.

The wing back on the weak side Lichtsteiner (26) drops back (further back than No.11) which enables him to create a numerical advantage (4 v 3) for Juventus in case the white No.2 passes forwards.

Contesting the New Man in Possession Aggressively (1)

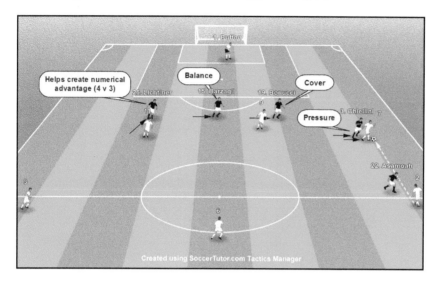

Before the ball is directed to white No.7, the 3 Juve centre backs need to be aware of the tactical situation.

Chiellini (3) moves to contest the new man in possession (7) aggressively. This is because Bonucci (19) provides cover and Juventus' right wing back Lichtsteiner (26) helps create a numerical advantage at the back by making a 4 man defence.

If No.7 dropped even deeper, Chiellini would still have followed the movement as the tactical situation favours this action.

Contesting the New Man in Possession Aggressively (2)

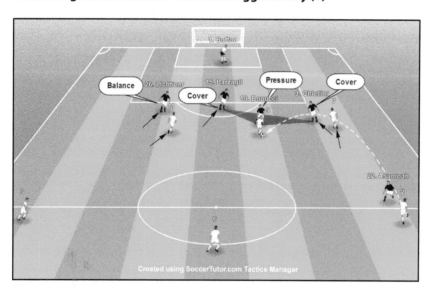

If the ball is passed to No.9, Bonucci moves to contest him aggressively.

Bonucci is able to do this because Barzagli provides cover and the wing back on the weak side Lichtsteiner's (26) starting position enables him to help create a numerical advantage at the back.

Defending Against 3 Narrow Forwards: Ball Near the Sideline (Wing Back in Ineffective Position)

If the Juventus wing back on the weak side was positioned higher up the pitch, the 3 centre backs would react differently to the previous examples, as they would have to adjust to the new tactical situation.

Ineffective Positioning of the Wing Back On the Weak Side When the Ball is Near the Sideline

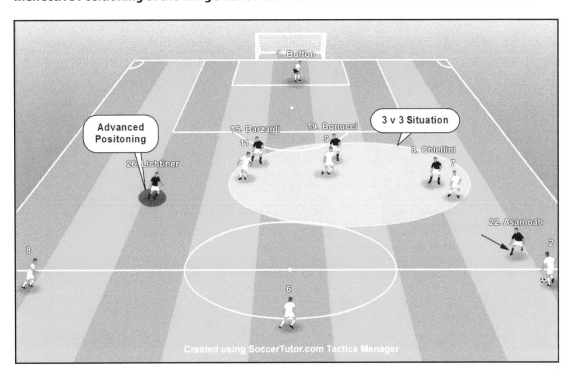

The 3 Juventus centre backs have direct opponents to mark in a 3 v 3 situation because the wing back on the weak side (26) is in an advanced position.

Playing for Time Against the New Man in Possession

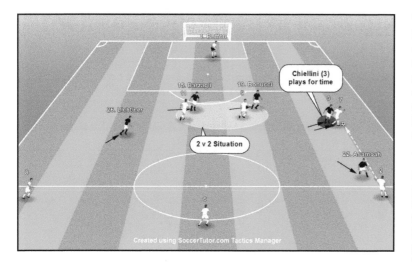

The ball is passed to white No.7. The Juventus defenders communicate and help Chiellini (3) to read the tactical situation. He doesn't move to contest the new ball carrier aggressively because if No.7 beats him in the duel the opposition will outnumber Juventus.

If No.7 drops into a deeper position, Chiellini should let him go and stay close to the other defenders. The best solution for Chiellini is playing for time as this allows Lichtsteiner (26) to recover into a more effective position and create a numerical advantage for Juve at the back.

Switching to Contest the Man in Possession Aggressively

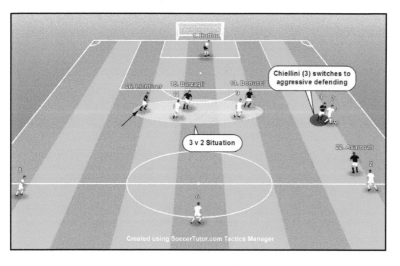

The wing back on the weak side (Lichtsteiner) recovers into a good defensive position and helps create a numerical advantage at the back (3 v 2).

In this situation Chiellini (3) can now contest the man in possession aggressively and try to win the ball instead of playing for time.

If Chiellini (3) is not able to observe Lichtsteiner's recovery into a good position, there should be coaching from his teammates.

Defending Against 3 Narrow Forwards: Ball in the Centre (Wing Back in Effective Position)

When the ball was directed from a player near the sideline towards the centre, the reaction of the defenders to a potential pass towards one of the forwards depended on the position of the wing back on the weak side.

Deep and Effective Positioning of the Wing Back On the Weak Side

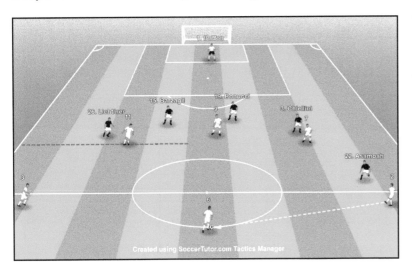

The diagram shows the starting positions of the players as soon as the white centre midfielder (6) receives the pass coming from the side.

The position of the Juventus wing back on the weak side (Lichtsteiner - No.26) is effective as he is behind the white No.11.

Good Positioning Enables the Defenders to Contest the New Man in Possession Aggressively

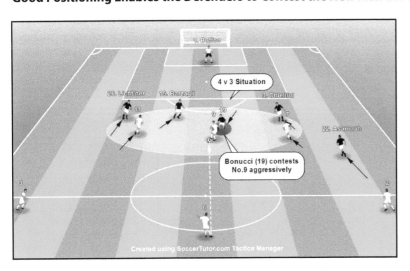

When the white No.6 decides to pass to No.9, Bonucci (19) moves forwards quickly to put pressure on the ball aggressively. This reaction is favourable because Juve have a numerical advantage at the back and there are 3 defenders ready to provide cover for Bonucci.

The players would react in the same way if the white No.6 had passed towards either No.11 or No.7.

Coaching the Juventus 3-5-2: Defending

Defending Against 3 Narrow Forwards: Ball in the Centre (Wing Back in Ineffective Position)

If the wing back on the weak side was positioned higher up the pitch and was unable to help create a numerical advantage at the back immediately, the 3 defenders' reaction had to be adjusted to the new tactical situation.

Ineffective Positioning of the Wing Back On the Weak Side When the Ball is in the Centre

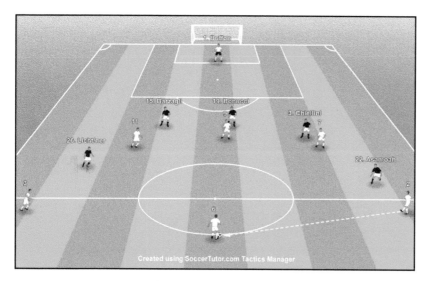

As soon as the ball is passed to No.6 this time, the position of the wing back is not good as he is higher up the pitch than in the previous situation and there is a 3 v 3 situation at the back for Juventus.

Playing for Time Against the New Man in Possession

The white centre midfielder (6) passes the ball to No.11. Barzagli (15) reads the tactical situation (or there is coaching from his teammates) and puts pressure on the new man in possession.

However, Barzagli's main aim is to play for time until Lichtsteiner (26) recovers into a more effective defensive position which will help create a numerical advantage at the back for Juventus.

Switching to Contest the Man in Possession Aggressively

Lichtsteiner recovers into a good defensive position and helps create a numerical advantage at the back (4 v 3).

In a situation like this Barzagli can now switch to a more aggressive way of contesting the player in possession to try and win the ball. He is safe in the knowledge that there is cover and good defensive balance behind him.

SESSION FOR THIS TACTICAL SITUATION (4 Practices)

1. Defending With the Wing Back On the Weak Side in an Effective Position (1)

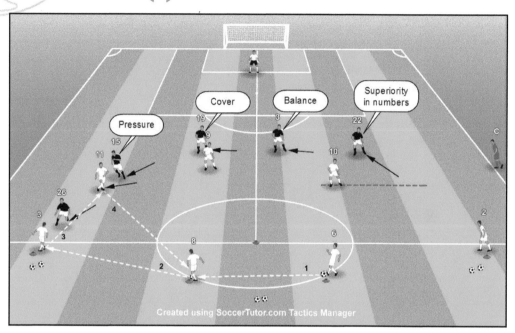

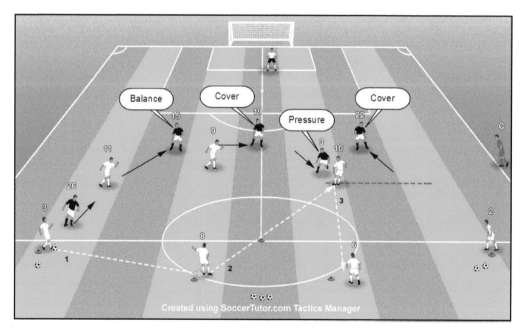

Objective

We work on how to defend in situations when the wing back on the weak side had an effective defensive position. This enabled the player closest to the ball to defend aggressively and try to win possession.

Description

We divide the pitch up into 2 halves so that the players are able to more easily recognise the weak and the strong sides. The 4 white midfielders are positioned by the red cones and pass the ball to each other.

The 3 black centre backs shift according to the position of the ball and mark the 3 narrow opposition forwards. The weak side's wing back (22) starts in line with the white forward on the weak side (10) in order to retain an effective position.

There are 2 variations within this practice:

Diagram 1

The pass towards the forwards can only be made by the wide midfielders (or wing/full backs) - No.2 and No.3. As soon as No.3 receives the ball, the strong side's wing back (black No.26) moves to apply pressure without blocking the potential pass.

When the pass is played to one of the forwards (No.11 in diagram), black No.15 applies pressure on the ball and the other defenders shift to take up the appropriate positions providing cover, balance and maintaining superiority in numbers. The coach corrects any mistakes in player movement or positioning.

The forward who receives (11) holds the ball for a couple of seconds and then passes back.

Diagram 2

The pass towards the forwards can only be made by the centre midfielders No.6 and No.8.

When the pass is played to one of the forwards (No.10 in diagram), No.3 applies pressure on the ball and the other defenders shift to take up the appropriate positions providing cover, balance and maintaining superiority in numbers. The coach corrects any mistakes in player movement or positioning.

The forward who receives (10) holds the ball for a couple of seconds and then passes back.

PROGRESSION

2. Defending With the Wing Back On the Weak Side in an Effective Position (2)

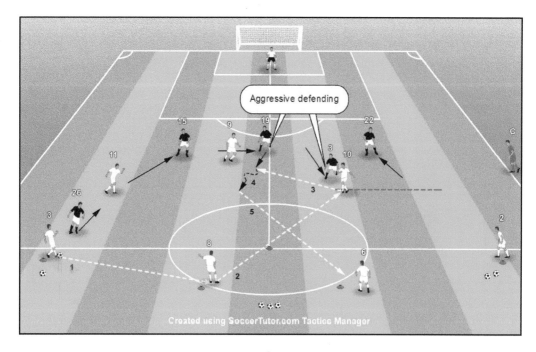

Objective

We work on how to defend in situations when the wing back on the weak side had an effective defensive position. This enabled the player closest to the ball to defend aggressively and try to win possession.

Description

This is a progression of the previous practice. As soon as the pass is made towards a forward from one of the midfielders, the white forwards try to attack and score within 10 seconds.

There are 2 variations within this practice as in the previous one - diagram 1 shows when passes to the forwards are only allowed from the wide players and diagram 2 shows when the passes are only allowed from the centre midfielders.

The defenders apply aggressive marking and try to win the ball, then make a clearance towards the white midfielders which is demonstrated in both diagram examples. Finally the defenders will then move forwards together in synchronisation.

Only the 3 white forwards (9, 10 and 11) are allowed to participate in the attack.

Coaching Points

1. The defenders need to be constantly moving to take up the appropriate positions according to the situation.

2. To defend against 3 forwards, one centre back must apply pressure on the ball and the other defenders need to provide cover, balance and retain a numerical advantage at the back.

VARIATION

3. Defending With the Wing Back On the Weak Side in an Ineffective Position (1)

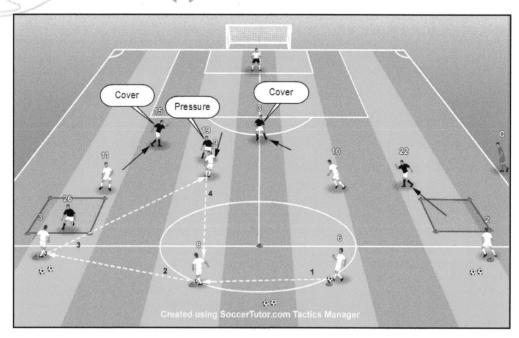

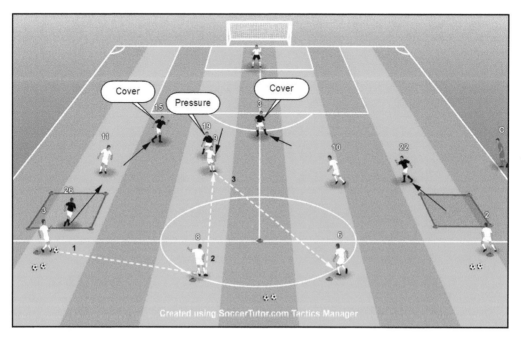

Objective

We work on how to defend in situations when the wing back on the weak side had poor positioning.

Description

We divide the pitch up into 2 halves so that the players are able to more easily recognise the weak and the strong side. The 4 white midfielders are positioned by the red cones and pass the ball to each other.

The 3 black centre backs shift according to the position of the ball and mark the 3 narrow opposition forwards. The wing back on the weak side (No.22 in diagram) always starts inside the red box (5 x 5 yards) no matter where the white forward is.

The whites do not try to score as the focus is on the black team reading the tactical situation in order to use the appropriate type of defending.

There are 2 variations within this practice:

Diagram 1

The pass towards the forwards can only be made by the wide midfielders (or wing/full backs) - No.2 and No.3. As soon as No.3 receives the ball, the wing back on the strong side (black No.26) moves to apply pressure without blocking the potential pass.

When the pass is played to one of the forwards (No.9 in diagram), the closest defender to the ball (19) moves to apply pressure in a passive way (as the wing back on the weak side is still in an ineffective position).

There needs to be good communication between the defenders so that the first defender knows to apply pressure passively initially and to then make sure he knows when the wing back has recovered so he can switch to aggressive defending. The coach corrects any mistakes in player movement or positioning.

The forward who receives (9) holds the ball for 2-6 seconds and then passes back.

Diagram 2

In diagram 2 the only difference is that the pass towards the forwards can only be made by the centre midfielders No.6 and No.8.

The forward who receives (9) holds the ball for 2-6 seconds and then passes back.

Coaching the Juventus 3-5-2: Defending

PROGRESSION

4. Defending With the Wing Back On the Weak Side in an Ineffective Position (2)

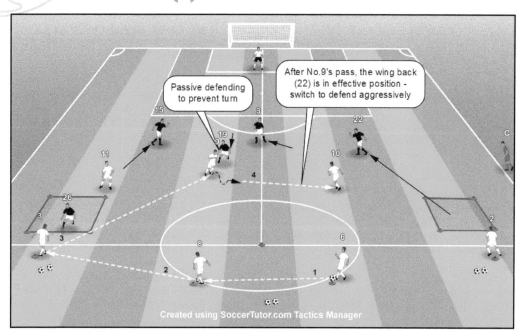

> Passive defending to prevent turn

> After No.9's pass, the wing back (22) is in effective position - switch to defend aggressively

> Passive defending to play for time until wing back (22) is in an effective position

Objective

We work on how to defend in situations when the wing back on the weak side had poor positioning.

Description

This is a progression of the previous practice. As soon as the pass is made towards a forward from one of the midfielders, the white forwards try to attack and score within 10 seconds.

There are 2 variations within this practice as in the previous one - diagram 1 shows when passes to the forwards are only allowed from the wide players and diagram 2 shows when the passes are only allowed from the centre midfielders.

The defenders have to react according to the tactical situation and play for time until the wing back on the weak side (22) recovers into an effective defensive position which creates a numerical advantage at the back.

When the wing back is out of position, the first defender uses passive defending, preventing the ball carrier from turning. Once the wing back on the weak side recovers into an effective position, then the black defenders try to win the ball and make a clearance towards the white midfielders. Finally the defenders move forwards together in synchronisation.

Only the 3 white forwards (9, 10 and 11) are allowed to participate in the attack.

Defending a Diagonal Pass to a Wide Forward Behind the Wing Back

A potential diagonal pass towards the space in behind the wing back was a difficult situation for Juventus to deal with, especially when the opposition played with 3 forwards.

Defending a Diagonal Pass Towards the Weak Side With the Wing Back in the Wrong Position

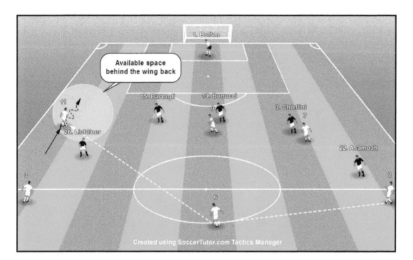

In this tactical situation Lichtsteiner (26) has a poor defensive position.

The worst scenario in this tactical situation is not a pass towards No.9 or No.7 (as shown in the previous examples).

The worst scenario for Juventus is a diagonal pass into the path of the wide forward (11) high up on the flank (the space behind Lichtsteiner).

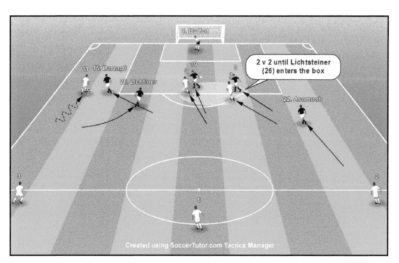

Barzagli (15) is the closest man to the white No.11 and moves across to the flank to close him down, aiming to play for time until Lichtsteiner (26) manages to get into a good defensive position by entering the penalty area (covering Barzagli's position) and creating a numerical advantage at the back.

If Lichtsteiner (26) didn't make this covering movement, there would be a 2 v 2 situation inside the penalty area, meaning the opposition would be much more likely to score.

In situations when the opposition players on the flank moved in synchronisation to create space, the defenders dealt with the situation according to the tactical context. If the wing back on the weak side had an effective position, Juventus could defend in the ways shown in the diagrams below:

Preventing the Opposition Creating Space On the Flank

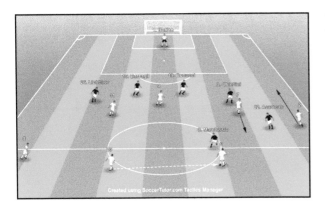

The white forward (7) drops deep in an attempt to receive to feet and create space on the flank at the same time. The white full back (2) makes a well timed run on the right flank to take advantage of the space created. In this situation Bonucci (19) provides cover to Chiellini (3) and there is already a numerical advantage for Juventus at the back (4 v 3).

If we followed the tactics used in the analysis on previous pages, Chiellini would follow his direct opponent (7). However Asamoah's (22) position is poor so the reaction needs to be different.

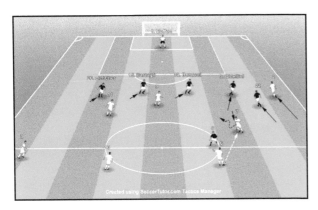

Chiellini (3) reads the tactical situation that the left wing back Asamoah's (22) position is poor and chooses not to follow No.7. Instead he drops back to cover the white No.2's run while No.7 receives and turns in a deep position.

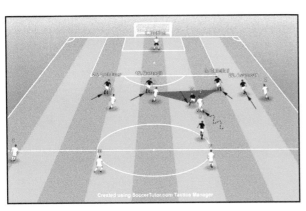

The man in possession (7) moves forward with the ball and the Juventus defenders drop back to make themselves more compact and give Asamoah (22) time to recover into an effective position.

When the defenders manage to get compact and Asamoah is in a good position, the closest player to the man in possession (No.19 Bonucci in the diagram) moves to close him down. The team is well balanced and the result is that there is no available space for the white No.2 to exploit high up the flank.

CHAPTER 2
MIDFIELD POSITIONING

MIDFIELD POSITIONING

In regards to the defensive positioning of Juventus' midfielders, things were rather simple. In situations when there was a numerical advantage at the back they defended the space instead of tracking their direct opponents and looked to maintain the correct shape for every second during the match.

However, in situations when the opposition midfielders moved into advanced positions and an equality or inferiority in numbers was created at the back, they had to follow the movements of the opposition forwards. This was not in order to mark the forwards, but to get closer to the defenders and be able to compensate for the tactical situation.

When the team's aim was to defend passively, the midfielders looked to narrow the potential passing lanes and block the passes towards the forwards. In addition, retaining cohesion (short distances between the defenders and midfielders) enabled them to apply double marking against the opposition forwards.

During the pressing application, in some cases, the attacking midfielders had to move forward to put pressure on the opposing full backs. This triggered a chain reaction for the rest of the midfielders who all moved towards the strong side.

Midfield Shape and Positioning to Prevent Through Passes From the Defenders

When the ball was in an opposition defender's possession and the team's aim was to defend in a passive way, the midfielders sought to take up the appropriate positions to block the potential through passes. This could be achieved by retaining the correct shape and compactness as well as maintaining a safety distance from the opposition defenders.

The midfielders tried to both block the through passes and mark the potential receivers near the ball zone.

Midfield Shape and Positioning When the Ball is in the Centre

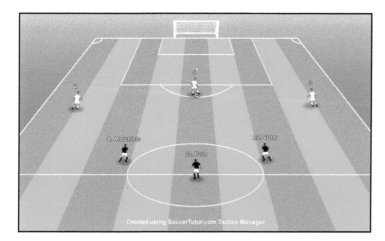

The ball is in the opposition's centre back's (5) possession. The 3 Juventus midfielders (8, 21 and 23) take up positions according to the position of the ball, retaining the correct shape to stay compact. They also retain a safety distance from the opposition defenders.

With this positioning the Juventus midfielders are able to intercept any potential through passes.

Midfield Shape and Positioning When the Ball is Out Wide

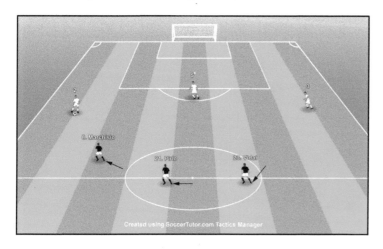

When the ball was near the sideline the 3 Juventus midfielders shifted towards the strong side.

Marchisio (8) who is on the strong side shifts across and forwards. Pirlo (21) and Vidal (23) stay in the same line together.

The Midfielders Drop Back When the Defender in Possession is Free of Marking

In situations when the opposition defender with the ball was free of marking and had plenty of space to take advantage of, the midfielders dropped back with two aims:

1.   To retain a safety distance and have enough time to react to a potential through pass.

2.   To give time to the forward closer to the player in possession to close him down.

The Opposition's Centre Back Moves Forward With the Ball

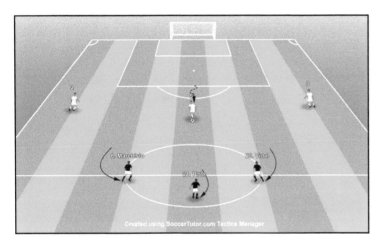

If the middle centre back (5) was the one who moved forward with the ball, the Juventus midfielders dropped back and retained their shape.

The attacking midfielders (Marchisio and Vidal) converged towards the inside to block the potential through balls and all 3 midfielders dropped back.

The Opposition's Left/Right Centre Back Moves Forward With the Ball

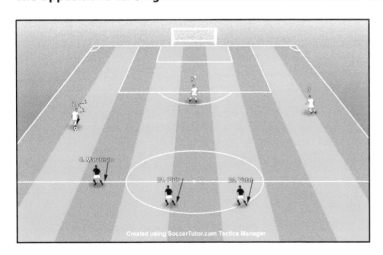

In this situation the right centre back (2) moves forward with the ball.

The Juventus midfielders drop back, get more compact and retain a safety distance from the defender at the same time as maintaining the correct shape.

The same reaction would have occurred against either centre back in a four man defence.

©SoccerTutor.com   *Coaching the Juventus 3-5-2: Defending*

SESSION FOR THIS TACTICAL SITUATION (2 Practices)

1. Retaining Shape and Cohesion to Block Through Passes in Midfield

Created using SoccerTutor.com Tactics Manager

Objective

The midfield three practice defending against attempted through balls from opposition defenders.

Description

We mark out 2 zones as shown. You can either play with 3 or 4 white defenders who are positioned inside the blue zone (10 yards x width of pitch). The defenders pass the ball between each other and wait for the right moment to try and play a through pass towards the 2 white players (9 and 11) inside the red zone (5 x 44 yards). A successful pass must be received within the red zone.

The black midfielders (8, 21 and 23) are positioned in front of the red zone and shift cohesively according to the position of the ball. They must stay compact, retain the correct shape and narrow the passing lanes so they can intercept the ball. They are not allowed to enter the red zone or the blue zone.

Coaching Points

1. Communication between the players is important so that they retain short distances between each other and collectively react to the changing situation.

2. The midfielders need to take advantage of the transmission phase (the time the ball takes to travel), using quick reactions to anticipate and intercept the ball.

PROGRESSION

2. Retaining Shape and a 'Safe Distance' to Block Through Passes in Midfield

Created using SoccerTutor.com Tactics Manager

Objective

The midfielders practice retaining a safe distance and blocking through passes from the opposition's defenders.

Description

This is a progression of the previous practice. The 2 marked zones are bigger - the blue zone is 15 yards x the width of the pitch and the red zone is 15 x 44 yards. This gives more time and space for the white defenders to move forward (or backward) and wait for the right time to attempt a through pass.

The black midfielders are in the red zone this time with 2 white forwards (9 and 11) who must stay behind them at all times. When the black midfielders drop back, the white forwards must also move back.

The 3 black midfielders (8, 21 and 23) aim to retain a safe distance and maintain a good shape so they have enough time to react when the passes are made. If they keep close distances between each other (compact), move in a cohesive way and display quick reactions to anticipate passes, they will intercept the ball more easily.

Defending Against the Opposition Midfielders

When the midfielders defended against the opposition midfielders who were in possession, their aim was to put pressure on the ball, as well as to provide cover and balance according to the tactical situation.

Horizontal Shifts of the Midfielders

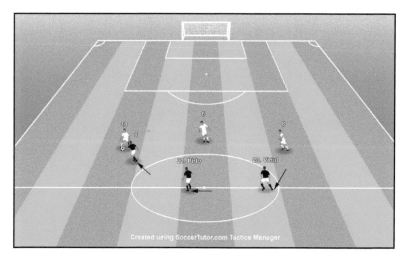

The ball is in the opposition midfielder's (10) possession.

Marchisio (8) puts pressure on No.10, while Pirlo (21) provides cover and Vidal (23) provides balance.

Good Positioning Allows the Midfielders to Contest the New Man in Possession Aggressively

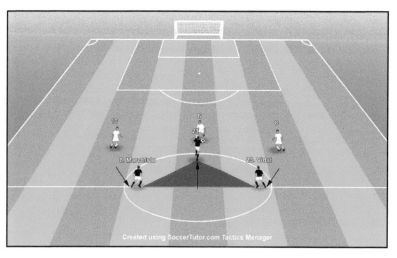

The ball is in the opposition defensive midfielder's (6) possession.

Pirlo (21) is the one who puts pressure on the ball while the other two midfielders provide cover and create a defensive triangle.

SESSION FOR THIS TACTICAL SITUATION (2 Practices)

1. Defending Against the Opposition Midfield (Pressure, Cover and Balance)

Created using SoccerTutor.com Tactics Manager

Objective

To practice defending in the central midfield zone (3 v 3) - pressure, cover and balance.

Description

The 3 black midfielders play against 3 white midfielders inside a 20 x 44 yard area. The closest black player to the ball (No.8 in diagram) applies pressure and the other 2 provide cover and balance according to the situation. By keeping a good shape and staying compact they aim to prevent the opponents from running with the ball through the red end line.

If the black team win the ball they have 5 seconds to dribble over the opposite red end line. If a team scores by dribbling over a red line or the ball goes out of play, everyone goes back to the same starting positions.

Coaching Points

1. The players need to have good organisation and communication in midfield; one player presses the ball.

2. It is important to retain short distances between each other and collectively react if an opposition player tries to dribble the ball in between them.

PROGRESSION

2. Defending Against the Opposition Midfield in a 3 v 3 End Zone Game

Created using SoccerTutor.com Tactics Manager

Objective

To practice defending in the central midfield zone (3 v 3) - pressure, cover and balance.

Description

In this progression of the previous practice we still play 3 v 3 in the same area, but we add 2 end zones (5 x 44 yards) and 6 mini goals in the positions shown.

The closest black player to the ball (No.8 in diagram) applies pressure and the other 2 provide cover and balance according to the situation. By keeping a good shape and staying compact they aim to prevent the opponents from running with the ball through the red end line. If the black team win the ball they have 5 seconds to dribble over the opposite red end line.

Once any player has dribbled through the red end line into an end zone they score 1 point and they score an additional point if they successfully score in one of the mini goals. When a team scores a point or the ball goes out of play, everyone goes back to the same starting positions.

Restriction

Players must shoot immediately after entering the white end zones (with their first touch within it).

CHAPTER 3
DEFENDING WITH THE REAR BLOCK (DEFENDERS AND MIDFIELDERS)

DEFENDING WITH THE REAR BLOCK (DEFENDERS AND MIDFIELDERS)

On the diagrams in this chapter we show how the rear block made of the defenders and the midfielders worked in collaboration when defending against various formations. The main aim of the block was to retain a numerical advantage at the back. This was obtained mainly with the contribution of the wing back on the weak side.

In some situations however, it was the midfielders who had to compensate for the equality or inferiority in numbers at the back. So when it was needed one of the midfielders dropped back close to the defenders and helped so that time could be given to the appropriate player to get back into an effective position.

Except for compensating for the equality or inferiority in numbers at the back, the block had to make sure that it kept the appropriate shape. The correct shape was important because when the players took up the appropriate positions they could block the through passes, provide support (mainly to the wing backs), balance and cover for each other.

Finally the midfielders together with the defenders (working as a block) had to keep a compact formation. The compactness meant a reduced distance between the two lines. This had a triple effect:

1. There was limited space for the opponents to take advantage of.

2. The defenders wouldn't have to move away from their staring positions when they followed the forwards.

3. The midfielders didn't have to cover long distances if they had to compensate for a numerical equality at the back.

DEFENDING WITH THE REAR BLOCK AGAINST THE 3-4-3

DEFENDING WITH THE REAR BLOCK AGAINST THE 3-4-3

Defending With the Rear Block Against the 3-4-3 Formation (1)

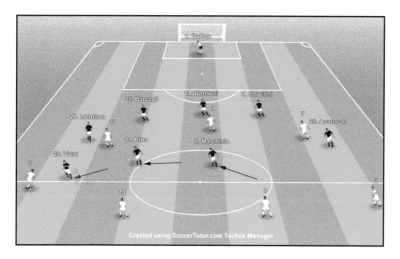

Juventus are defending against a team using the 3-4-3 formation. Against this specific formation the team had to make some adjustments as there was a 3 v 3 situation at the back. Lichtsteiner (26) dropped into a deeper and more defensive position than the other wing back. This created a 4 man defence against the 3 forwards.

Vidal (23) shifted slightly towards the right to be able to contest the opposition's wing back if he had the ball. Lichtsteiner stays close to the defenders and helps retain a 4 v 3 numerical advantage at the back. The rest of the midfielders shift towards the strong side.

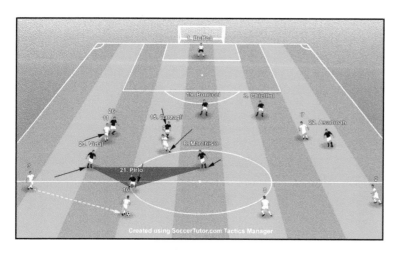

The pass is directed to the white midfielder (10). Pirlo (21) moves to put pressure on him while Vidal (23) and Marchisio (8) provide cover by creating a defensive triangle with the aim of blocking the potential through passes.

The white forward (9) moves towards the passing lane. Barzagli (15) reads the tactical situation and follows his movement (as the situation favours it) just in case No.10 manages to pass him the ball.

Coaching the Juventus 3-5-2: Defending

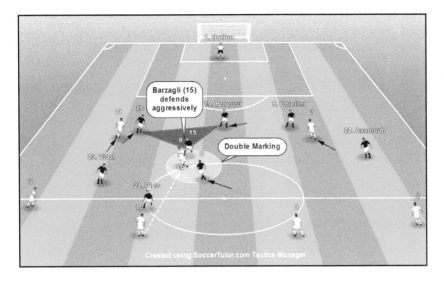

As soon as the ball is passed to No.9, Barzagli (15) puts pressure on him and prevents him from turning. At the same time Marchisio (8) turns and helps to double mark him from the inside.

The right wing back Lichtsteiner (26) drops back to provide cover and block a potential through ball and Bonucci (19) provides cover from the other side of Barzagli. A defensive triangle is created by these 3 players, as shown in the diagram.

Defending With the Rear Block Against the 3-4-3 Formation (2)

If the ball is played from white No.10 to No.8 instead of No.9, Marchisio (8) is the first player who puts pressure on the ball. The other two midfielders (21 and 23) shift towards the left.

The defenders also shift towards the left and retain short distances between each other. These short distances help them to pass the responsibility of marking from one player to the other easily. An opposition player only stays free for a couple of seconds before one of the defenders takes over his marking.

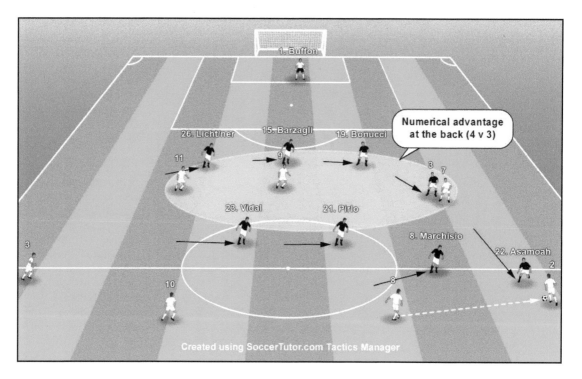

When the white No.8 passes to No.2, there is a synchronised shift of all the Juventus' defenders in the form of a chain reaction.

The left wing back Asamoah (22) takes advantage of the transmission phase (the time the ball takes to travel) and moves forward to put pressure on the new player in possession.

Marchisio provides support and the short distances between the defenders enable Chiellini (3) to move quickly forward and mark No.7 closely.

Barzagli (15) and Bonucci (19) move across in the same line behind. The right wing back Lichtsteiner (26) is the one who helps create a numerical advantage at the back. The midfielders have the correct shape as they take up positions behind the ball.

PRACTICE FOR THIS TACTICAL SITUATION

Defending With the Rear Block Against the 3-4-3 in a Functional Practice

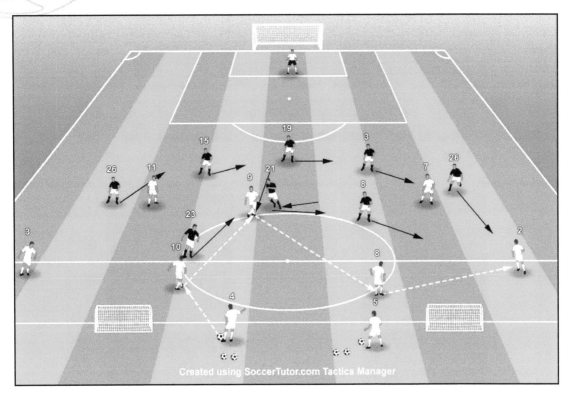

Created using SoccerTutor.com Tactics Manager

Description

The black team have 1 goalkeeper, 3 defenders and 5 midfielders (3-5 formation). They play against the white team who have 4 midfielders and 3 forwards (4-3 formation + 2 outside players who feed the ball in).

The whites (with the help of the outside players No.4 and No.5) look to attack successfully and score. The defending players (black team) try to block the through passes, apply double marking and when possible, win the ball. After gaining possession they must then score within 6-8 seconds into one of the two mini goals. This practice can be used against various formations.

Coaching Points

1. The black team must take up the appropriate positions according to the position of the ball.

2. The player closest to the ball needs to put pressure on the ball carrier, while the others provide cover and balance. This requires good communication and coaching from the players.

3. The rear block (3-5 formation) must retain the correct shape and remain compact to block through passes.

4. It is very important that the players's defensive movements are synchronised.

DEFENDING WITH THE REAR BLOCK AGAINST THE 3-4-1-2

DEFENDING WITH THE REAR BLOCK AGAINST THE 3-4-1-2

If the opposition were using the 3-4-1-2 formation, putting pressure on the wing backs was mainly a job for the Juventus wing backs. This could result in both Lichtsteiner and Asamoah being in advanced positions and the wing back who was on the weak side would therefore not have enough time to recover quickly to provide immediate help to the 3 defenders.

In these situations the defensive midfielder Pirlo had to take up a deeper position in order to compensate for a potential 3 v 3 situation occurring at the back, most often due to the opposing No.10's advanced position. The Juventus defensive midfielder would keep an eye on the No.10 until the wing back on the weak side could recover into an effective position which enabled him to provide help and restore a numerical advantage at the back.

Defending With the Rear Block Against the 3-4-1-2

Defending With the Rear Block Against the 3-4-1-2 Formation

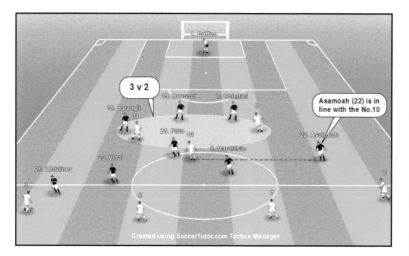

Lichtsteiner (26) puts pressure on the wing back No.3.

Pirlo (21) takes up a deeper position than usual in order to compensate for the advanced positions of the wing backs in case No.10 moves into a forward position. There is a 3 v 2 situation at the back for Juve to ensure safety.

However, it is necessary for Asamoah (22) to be in an effective position in line with No.10 and not in a wide position, as he can see the full pitch (Pirlo cannot). With this positioning Asamoah can drop back immediately and create a numerical advantage at the back if No.10 moves further forward behind Pirlo.

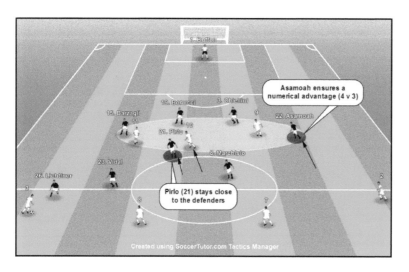

The white No.10 moves forward. If Pirlo (21) is unable to see him there is communication between the players.

Pirlo drops back but not to mark the No.10. It is so he can stay close to the defenders and provide help if necessary until the wing back on the weak side (Asamoah) drops back into an effective defensive position.

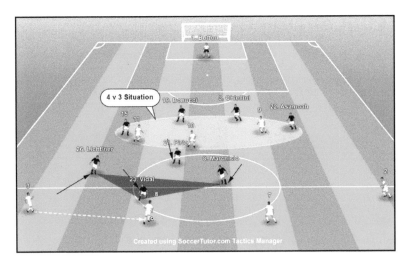

The ball is passed to white No.8 and Vidal (23) puts pressure on him. Lichtsteiner and Marchisio (8) help form a defensive triangle to block any potential through passes.

Pirlo moves a few yards forward as the left wing back Asamoah has an effective position to help create a 4 v 3 numerical advantage at the back.

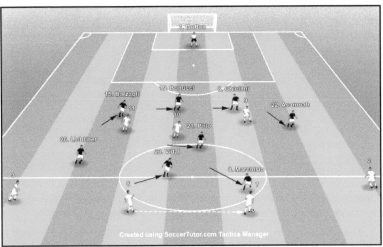

When the ball is passed across to white No.7, Marchisio (8) moves to close him down.

Vidal (23) and Pirlo (21) shift towards the left and so do all the rest of the Juventus players (cohesive and compact rear block).

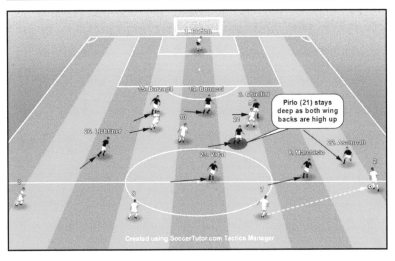

As soon as the ball is passed to white No.2 and Asamoah (22) moves forward to close him down, Pirlo (21) has to evaluate the tactical situation.

If the wing back on the weak side (Lichtsteiner) is still in an advanced position, Pirlo (21) stays close to the defenders until Lichtsteiner (26) is able to drop into an effective defensive position.

Coaching the Juventus 3-5-2: Defending

SESSION FOR THIS TACTICAL SITUATION (3 Practices)

1. Defensive Reactions Against the 3-4-1-2 With Equality in Numbers at the Back (1)

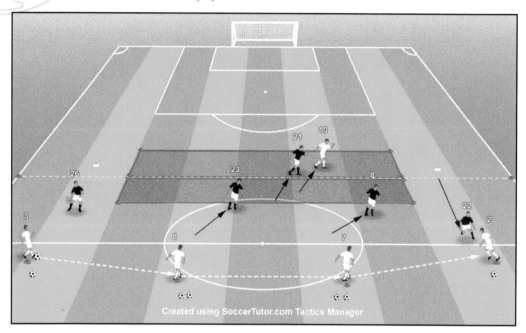

Created using SoccerTutor.com Tactics Manager

Objective

Players learn to compensate for the potential equality in numbers at the back by reading the tactical situation. This practice is centred around the defensive midfielder who must read the tactical situation.

Description

We mark out a line across the pitch and 2 zones (5 x 44 yards each). The white No.10 and the black defensive midfielder (21) start inside the red zone while the other 2 black midfielders (23 and 8) are outside of it.

We have 4 white players positioned by the red cones and the No.10 can move freely across both the zones while his teammates pass the ball to each other. The black defensive midfielder (21) has to evaluate the tactical situation and take the appropriate reaction. The other black midfielders use pressure, cover and balance. If the white No.10 is inside the blue zone and the wing back on the weak side (No.26 in the diagram) is beyond the white line, then the defensive midfielder (21) drops back into the blue zone - as shown in the diagram.

If the white No.10 is inside the blue zone and the wing back on the weak side is beyond the white line, then the defensive midfielder (21) stays in the red zone. He has the same reaction if the white No.10 is inside the red zone and the wing back on the weak side is level or behind the white line.

Coaching Points

1. The defensive midfielder needs to drop back at the right moment after judging the tactical situation.

2. The other players need to take up the right positions according to the ball position - pressure/cover/balance.

PROGRESSION

2. Defensive Reactions Against the 3-4-1-2 With Equality in Numbers at the Back (2)

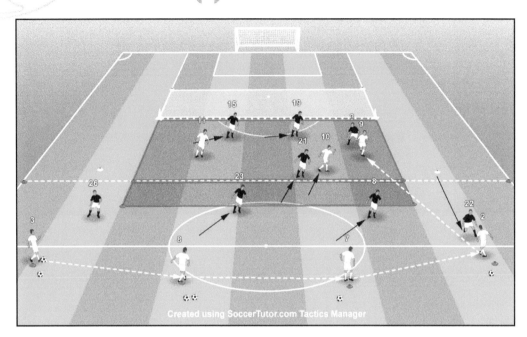

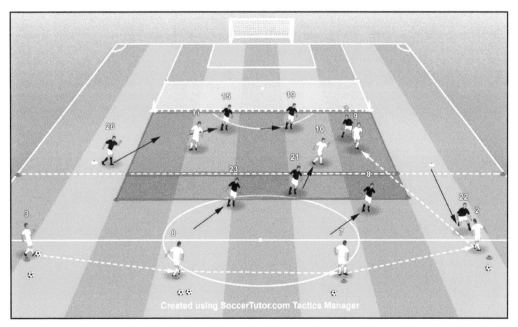

Objective

Players learn to compensate for the potential equality in numbers at the back by reading the tactical situation.

Description

This is a progression of the previous practice. This time 3 defenders are added for the black team (15, 19 and 3) and we have 2 white forwards (9 and 10) who are all positioned inside the now larger blue zone.

The white midfielders pass the ball to each other and then pass to one of the forwards inside the blue zone. The white No.10 moves freely inside both zones (blue and red). The whites aim to dribble the ball through the red line or receive a pass inside the yellow zone. The offside rule is applied throughout.

The black defensive midfielder (21) has to evaluate the tactical situation and take the appropriate reaction again by dropping back (diagram 1) or staying inside the red zone (diagram 2). This decision is always according to the position of the wing back on the weak side (No.26) - as explained in the previous practice.

If the defensive midfielder (21) makes a bad decision his teammates inside the blue zone will have to play with equality in numbers against the opposition forwards (3 v 3 situation).

The black defending team try to win the ball, make a clearance towards the white midfielders before quickly stepping up together.

This wing back on the weak side (26) can enter the blue zone to help his teammates after the pass towards the forwards is made, but only if his starting position was behind the white line (diagram 2).

Progression

A goalkeeper is added for the defending team and the whites aim to score (unopposed) after dribbling the ball through the red end line or after receiving a pass inside the white zone.

Restrictions

1. The white No.10 and the black defensive midfielder (21) are not allowed to enter the blue zone after the pass towards the forwards is made.
2. The other centre midfielders (23 and 8) take up the appropriate positions but they do not try to block the through passes.

PROGRESSION

3. Defending With the Rear Block Against the 3-4-1-2 in a Functional Practice

Created using SoccerTutor.com Tactics Manager

Objective

To develop tactical qualities; Taking up appropriate positions according to the ball position, putting pressure on the ball, providing cover/balance, retaining shape and compactness with synchronised movements.

Description

The black midfielders and defenders (3-5 formation) play against a white team using a 4-1-2 formation (+2 outside players No.4 and No.5). The whites (with the help of the outside players) try to attack and score.

The defending players (black team) try to block the through passes, apply double marking when possible, win the ball and counter attack to score in one of the two mini goals within 6-8 seconds.

ASSESSMENT:

These practices can be adjusted to defend against all different formations.

DEFENDING WITH THE REAR BLOCK AGAINST THE 3-5-2

DEFENDING WITH THE REAR BLOCK AGAINST THE 3-5-2

When defending against the 3-5-2 formation, things were quite simple for Juventus. The 3 defenders only had to deal with 2 forwards (numerical advantage of 3 v 2), unless there was a forward movement from one of the midfielders. Therefore the wing backs did not have to drop into very deep positions.

Defending With the Rear Block Against the 3-5-2 Formation (1)

The white No.7 has the ball and the left wing back Asamoah (22) puts pressure on him.

The rear block is well organised and balanced.

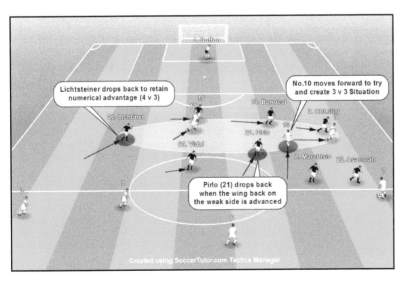

The white No.10 decides to move forward. As the movement takes place in front of Pirlo (21), he is the one who drops back a few yards.

Pirlo gets closer to the defenders and makes sure Juventus are not left with a 3 v 3 situation at the back.

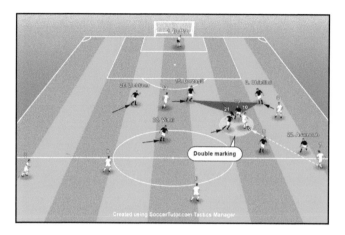

As the ball is directed to No.10, Bonucci (19) puts him under pressure and Pirlo (21) moves close to help double mark him. Barzagli (15) and Chiellini (3) provide cover and Lichtsteiner (26) helps keep the line balanced.

Pirlo's double marking is applied with two aims:

1. To win the ball immediately,

2. Allow time for the wing back on the weak side (Lichtsteiner) to drop back and create a numerical advantage at the back again.

Defending With the Rear Block Against the 3-5-2 Formation (2)

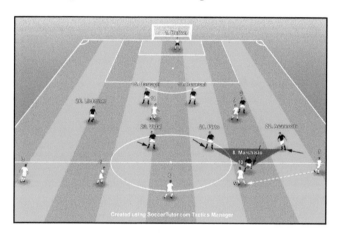

In this situation the white No.7 passes inside to No.10. Marchisio (8) puts him under pressure, Pirlo provides cover and Vidal (23) provides balance.

These 3 Juventus midfielders create a defensive triangle to block any potential through passes.

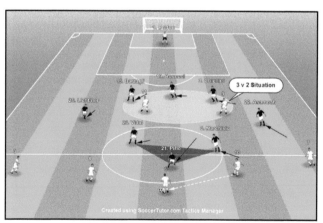

As soon as the pass is played to No.6, Pirlo is the first defender and Vidal (23) together with Marchisio (8) create a defensive triangle to block any potential through passes.

The Juventus defenders all shift towards the right side.

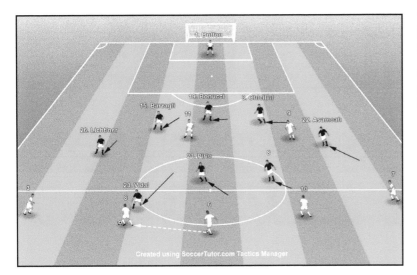

The white No.8 receives the ball and Vidal puts him under pressure.

All of the other Juventus players shift towards the right.

Finally the ball reaches No.3 out wide. All of the Juventus players shift across again towards the right.

Barzagli (15) stays close to the other defenders ready to provide help while the wing back on the weak side (Asamoah) is ready to move back and take up an effective position in defence.

Vidal (23) provides support to Lichtsteiner (26) and the other midfielders retain good shape.

ASSESSMENT:

Against this specific formation Juventus start with a 3 v 2 situation at the back. A problem can arise if an opposition midfielder moves into an advanced position and makes it 3 v 3.

The practices for other formations included in this book can be easily adapted so that you can practice defensive movements and cohesion against the 3-5-2 formation.

DEFENDING WITH THE REAR BLOCK AGAINST THE 4-2-3-1

DEFENDING WITH THE REAR BLOCK AGAINST THE 4-2-3-1

When the opposition used the 4-2-3-1 formation their wingers were usually in wide positions. There was also a centre forward and an attacking midfielder. The attacking midfielder's aim was to take advantage of the space between the defensive and midfield line. As there was one more player (attacking midfielder) who joined the attack compared to the 3-4-3 formation, the rear block of Juventus had to ensure that a numerical advantage at the back was maintained, otherwise situations where there was an equality in numbers (4 v 4) could often occur.

When defending against the 4-2-3-1, Juventus had to make certain adjustments in order to retain a numerical advantage at the back. These adjustments depended on which player put pressure on the opposition's full back. Against this specific system, in most situations, this was a job for either the wing back or the attacking midfielder. The positioning of the opposition's attacking midfielder also determined in what way Juventus would ensure a numerical superiority at the back. In the diagrams to follow we show analysis for how this was achieved.

Defending With the Rear Block Against the 4-2-3-1 Formation (1)

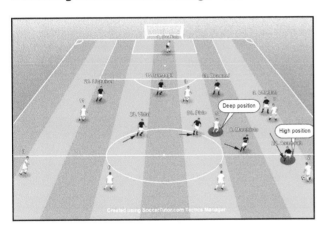

The left wing back Asamoah (22) puts pressure on the full back (2) in possession. Marchisio (8) provides support and blocks the potential through pass, while Chiellini (3) has a double aim; to provide cover for Asamoah (22) and mark No.7.

Pirlo (21) is positioned behind Marchisio (8) to control No.10 who is in a deep position. As Asamoah (22) is high up the pitch, the wing back on the weak side Lichtsteiner (26) is in a deep position. This keeps the formation compact, retaining a good shape and creating a numerical advantage (4 v 3) at the back.

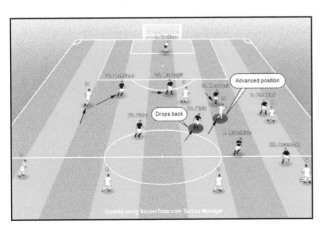

The white No.10 moves into a more advanced position between the lines. Bonucci (19) moves to mark him as he is a potential receiver.

The white No.10's movement creates a 4 v 4 situation at the back for Juventus, so Pirlo moves a couple of yards back - not with the aim of following and marking No.10, but in order to be closer to the defenders and be ready in a position to support them.

Defending With the Rear Block Against the 4-2-3-1 Formation (2)

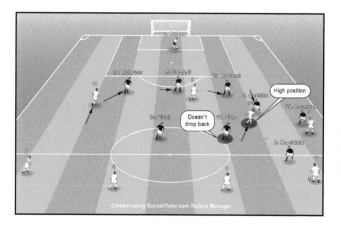

Here we show a different way of dealing with the same situation. Marchisio (8) is the player who puts pressure on the full back (2) this time. The rest of the midfielders retain a good shape with Pirlo (21) in position to block a potential through pass.

Even though the white No.10 is in an advanced position, Pirlo (21) doesn't have to drop back at all. This is because both wing backs are in deep positions and there is still a numerical advantage (5 v 4) at the back for Juventus.

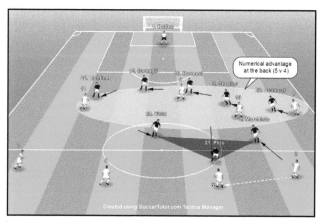

The full back passes to No.8. Pirlo (21) is the closest to the new ball carrier and moves to close him down.

The two attacking midfielders Marchisio (8) and Vidal (23) provide cover by forming a defensive triangle behind Pirlo.

Juve retain a numerical advantage at the back (5 v 4) despite the white No.10's advanced position.

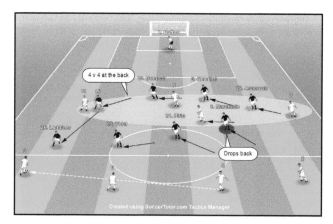

No.8 passes to the left back (3) and Lichtsteiner (26) takes advantage of the transmission phase (the time the ball takes to travel) to close the new man in possession down. Lichtsteiner is able to move forwards because the other wing back (Asamoah) is in an effective defensive position.

Barzagli (15) takes over No11's marking and Vidal (23) drops into a supporting position. As the white No.10 is in an advanced position behind the midfield line and Pirlo (21) cannot see him, Marchisio (8) drops back a few yards back to control him and compensate for the equality in numbers at the back (4 v 4). The block is well organised and difficult to break through.

Coaching the Juventus 3-5-2: Defending

Defending With the Rear Block Against the 4-2-3-1 Formation (3)

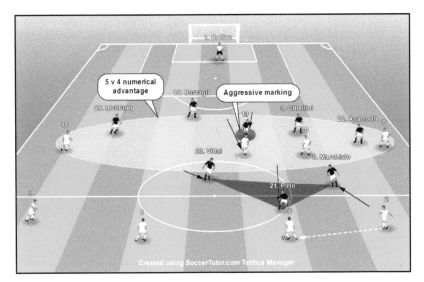

In this example the pass is directed to white No.8. Pirlo (21) is the closest and moves to close down the new ball carrier. Marchisio (8) and Vidal (23) provide cover by forming a defensive triangle to block potential through passes.

The white forward (9) drops back to receive in the available space created by Pirlo's advanced position. If there is an available passing lane towards him, Bonucci (19) follows his movement as the circumstances favour aggressive marking (there is a numerical advantage at the back).

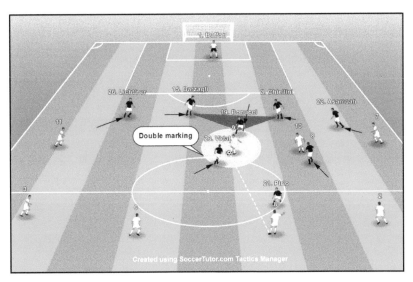

No.8 passes to the forward (9) and he is immediately put under pressure from Bonucci (19) and Vidal (23) who apply double marking.

Variation - **The Weak Side's Full Back is in an Advanced Position**

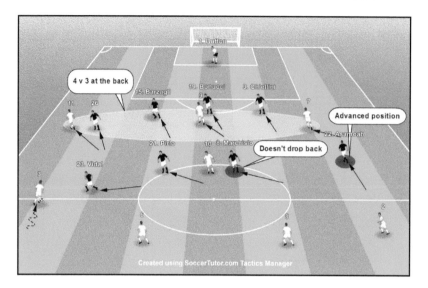

In a similar situation to the previous one, Asamoah is in an advanced position. In this case Lichtsteiner has to wait until Vidal moves to close No.3 down in order for numerical superiority to be retained. However, until Vidal closes the man in possession down, there is an open ball situation, so the defenders move back to prevent the forwards from receiving a pass behind their back. As No.10 is not in an advanced position and there is a 4 v 3 situation at the back, Marchisio doesn't have to drop further back.

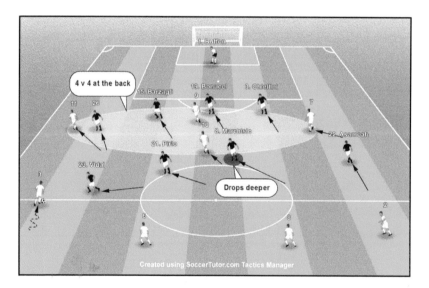

In another similar situation, No.10 moves forward and behind the midfielders. Marchisio reads the tactical situation (or there is coaching between the players) and drops close to the defenders.

As soon as Asamoah drops into an effective defensive position, Marchisio can move in a more advanced position.

SESSION FOR THIS TACTICAL SITUATION (2 Practices)

1. Defensive Reactions to Retain a Numerical Superiority When Closing Down the Full Back Against the 4-2-3-1 (1)

YELLOW CONE:
Wing Back Closes

BLUE CONE:
Att. Mid. Closes

©SoccerTutor.com

Coaching the Juventus 3-5-2: Defending

Objective

We work with the midfielders on their movements to prevent a numerical equality being created at the back and improve their synchronisation when defending against the 4-2-3-1 formation.

Description

This practice is designed to create two tactical situations that the midfielders have to recognise and then use the appropriate reaction.

We mark out 2 zones as shown. The No.10 is inside the yellow zone (2 x 44 yards) and moves freely to the right or left. The two white full backs (2 and 3) hold one yellow cone and one blue cone. The defending team's wing backs (26 and 22) wear yellow bibs and the attacking midfielders (23 and 8) wear blue bibs.

The practice starts with the white players by the red cones who pass to each other. The defending team's players shift according to the position of the ball. When a white full back receives the ball (No.2 in diagram) they raise one of the cones. This is the signal for which player should put pressure on the ball.

If the full back (2) raises the yellow cone, the wing back (22) closes him down (diagram 1). In this situation one of the midfielders (depending on the white No.10's position) has to drop into the blue zone (5 x 44 yards). In diagram 1 this is the defensive midfielder (21).

If the full back raises the blue cone, the attacking midfielder (No.8 in diagram) puts pressure on the ball (diagram 2). In this situation none of the midfielders drop back into the blue zone as both wing backs are in deep positions. If an attacking midfielder (23 or 8) puts pressure on the white full back, then the other midfielders just shift towards the strong side as shown in the diagram.

Coaching Points

1. To make sure they use the right reaction, the midfielders should inform each other about No.10's position.
2. If the wing back puts pressure on the ball, one of the midfielders (depending on No.10's position) needs to drop back at the right moment which simulates helping to retain a numerical advantage at the back for his team.

Coaching the Juventus 3-5-2: Defending

PROGRESSION

2. Defensive Reactions to Retain a Numerical Superiority When Closing Down the Full Back Against the 4-2-3-1 (2)

Description

In this progression, we add 2 black defenders (15 and 3) and 1 white forward (9) who are all positioned inside the blue zone (10 x 44 yards). The white No.10 is positioned inside the red zone.

The white midfielders and full backs pass the ball to each other and then pass to one of the forwards inside the red or blue zone. The whites aim to dribble the ball through the red line or receive a pass inside the yellow zone.

The black defensive midfielder (21) and the attacking midfielder on the weak side (23) have to evaluate the tactical situation and one of them has to drop back into the red zone depending on the white No.10's position. This is so that they can help the defenders and create a 3 v 2 numerical advantage. The defending team try to win the ball and then make a clearance towards the white midfielders/full backs, before quickly stepping up together.

Restrictions

1. Only the wing backs are allowed to move to close down the opposition full back with the ball.
2. The black midfielders (8, 21 and 23) do not try to block the through passes.
3. The defenders are not allowed to enter the yellow zone and the offside rule is applied throughout.

Progression: A goalkeeper is added for the defending team and the white team try to score (unopposed) after dribbling the ball through the red end line or after receiving a pass inside the yellow zone.

DEFENDING WITH THE REAR BLOCK AGAINST THE 4-4-2

DEFENDING WITH THE REAR BLOCK AGAINST THE 4-4-2

If the rear block were facing a team using the 4-4-2 formation, the player who moved forward to put pressure on the opposing full back was the attacking midfielder. Juventus would then be able to retain a numerical advantage at the back with 5 defenders against 4 opposing players (2 forwards and 2 wingers). However, a problem could arise if one of the opposition midfielders moved into an advanced position to make it 5 v 5.

Defending With the Rear Block Against the 4-4-2 Formation (1)

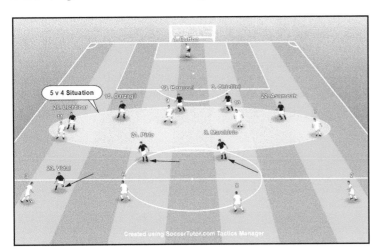

In this example there is a 5 v 4 situation at the back (numerical advantage) and the attacking midfielder Vidal (23) pushes forwards to close down the opposing left back (3).

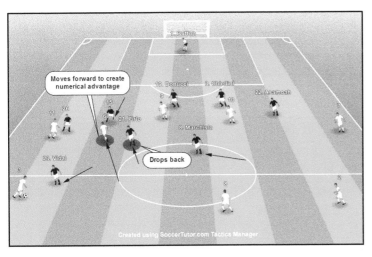

The white centre midfielder (6) moves into an advanced position and creates a 5 v 5 situation at the back for Juventus.

Pirlo (the closest midfielder to see No.6's movement) drops a few yards back to compensate for this. Marchisio (8) also drops into a balanced position in the centre of the pitch.

The right centre back Barzagli (15) moves forwards to control No.6 without moving away from his position to provide cover for the right wing back Lichtsteiner (26).

Coaching the Juventus 3-5-2: Defending

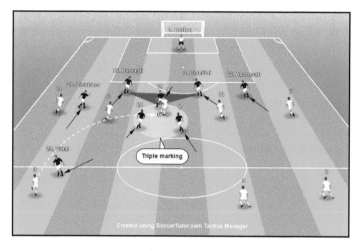

The white left back (3) plays a long pass towards the forward (9). Bonucci (19) puts him under pressure and prevents him from turning.

Pirlo (21) and Marchisio (8) provide help by dropping back and trying to apply triple marking.

Barzagli (15) and Chiellini (3) move inside into covering positions.

The white team's attacking move is blocked and they are unable to take advantage of the equality in numbers.

Defending With the Rear Block Against the 4-4-2 Formation (2)

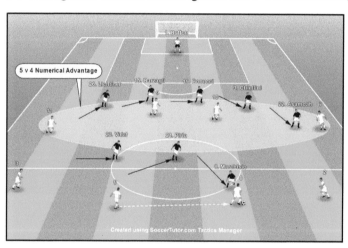

The pass is directed to No.8 and Marchisio moves forward to apply pressure on the new ball carrier.

The other Juventus midfielders retain the correct shape and the defenders shift towards the left side.

There is a 5 v 4 situation at the back.

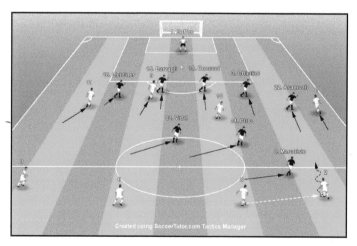

When the pass is played to the white right back (2) the new tactical situation can be dealt with in two ways. The first way is shown in this diagram.

The Juventus defenders drop back giving Marchisio (8) time to close the player in possession down. With this reaction the numerical advantage at the back is retained. However, Juventus have to defend deeper and the man in possession has enough time on the ball to search for an accurate pass.

The second way is shown in the three diagrams on the next page.

Coaching the Juventus 3-5-2: Defending

Defending With the Rear Block Against the 4-4-2 Formation (3)

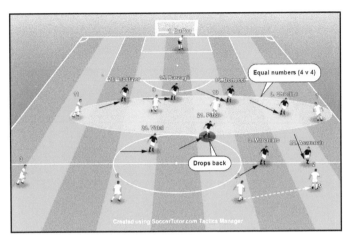

In this diagram we show a different reaction to the previous situation.

This time Asamoah (22) decides to move forward and close No.2 down by taking advantage of the transmission phase (the time the ball takes to travel).

The rest of the defenders shift across in the form of a chain reaction. Pirlo (21) drops back to be close to the defenders and gets ready to provide help if necessary and compensate for the equality in numbers (4 v 4) at the back.

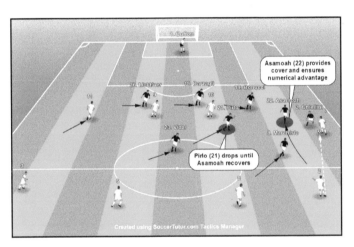

As soon as the ball is directed to the right midfielder (7), Chiellini (3) puts pressure on the ball with the aim of playing for time, while Pirlo (21) gets closer to the defenders.

With these actions safety is provided at the back as well as giving Asamoah (22) time to recover and take up a supporting position behind Chiellini (3).

As soon as this takes place the numerical superiority at the back is restored for Juventus. The rest of the defenders shift towards the strong side.

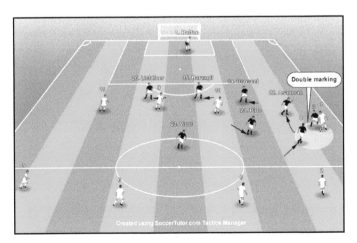

Finally, Asamoah (22) has taken up a covering position behind Chiellini (3) and Juventus have a spare player at the back again.

The rest of the defenders readjust their position according to the new situation and the line becomes more balanced.

At the same time Marchisio (8) helps Chiellini to double mark No.7 and Pirlo moves slightly forwards as there is no longer any need to be in a deep position.

PRACTICE FOR THIS TACTICAL SITUATION (VARIATION)

Defensive Reactions to Retain a Numerical Superiority When Closing Down the Full Back Against the 4-4-2

YELLOW CONE:
Wing Back Closes

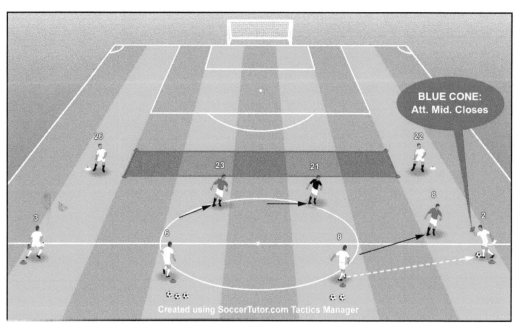

BLUE CONE:
Att. Mid. Closes

104

Objective

We work with the midfielders on their movements to prevent a numerical equality being created at the back and improve their synchronisation when defending against the 4-4-2 formation.

Description

This is a variation of the practice in the previous section for defending against the 4-2-3-1 formation. This time there is no player behind the midfielders.

The practice starts with the white midfielders and full backs positioned by the red cones. The black midfielders shift according to the position of the ball.

When a white full back receives the ball they raise either a yellow or blue cone. This is the signal for which the player should put pressure on the ball. If they raise the yellow cone, the wing back closes the full back down (diagram 1) and if they raise the blue cone, the attacking midfielder does (diagram 2).

If the wing back (No.22 in diagram) closes down the full back, the defensive midfielder (21) moves into the blue zone (diagram 1). If the attacking midfielder moves to close the full back down, the defensive midfielder stays outside of the zone (diagram 2).

DEFENDING WITH THE REAR BLOCK AGAINST THE 4-3-1-2

DEFENDING WITH THE REAR BLOCK AGAINST THE 4-3-1-2

This chapter is about how the rear block defended against the 4-3-1-2 formation. Their main aim was to retain a numerical advantage at the back. When they had to defend against two strikers a 3 v 2 situation was created. However in situations when the opposition's No.10 was in a position beyond the midfield line, one of the two wing backs (mainly the right wing back Lichtsteiner) had to take up a more defensive position in order to prevent a 3 v 3 situation from occurring.

Defending With the Rear Block Against the 4-3-1-2 Formation (1)

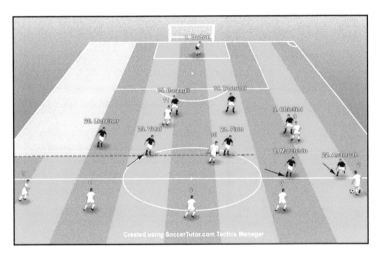

The left wing back Asamoah (22) puts pressure on the ball. Chiellini (3) marks the forward (9) who is in a deep position. The white No.10 is also in a deep position and the responsibility of marking him is passed to one of the midfielders.

Lichtsteiner (26) takes up a position which enables him to drop deeper and provide help to the other defenders (behind Juventus' deepest midfielder and not too wide in the white area). This is in case the white No.10 moves forward and in behind the midfield line. In that situation, Lichtsteiner (26) should be able to help the defence and prevent a 3 v 3 situation from occurring.

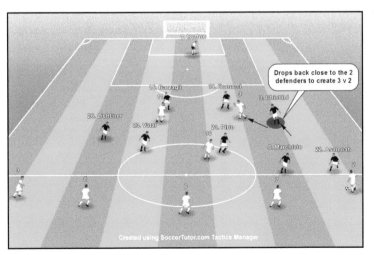

The white No.9 moves into a more advanced position. The responsibility of marking him is passed to Bonucci (19).

Bonucci coaches Chiellini (3) to drop a few yards back in order for safety and balance to be achieved. This also allows both Bonucci and Barzagli (15) to be able to aggressively contest No.11 or No.9 if the ball is passed to them.

Coaching the Juventus 3-5-2: Defending

Defending With the Rear Block Against the 4-3-1-2 Formation (2)

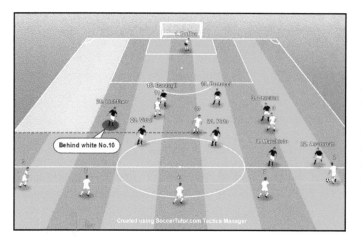

When the No.10 was in an advanced position as shown in this diagram, in order for Lichtsteiner (26) to be in an effective position he had to be positioned behind the No.10 and not too wide (not inside the highlighted white area).

This starting position for Lichtsteiner enabled him to help create a 4 v 3 situation at the back in case the No.10 moved further forward.

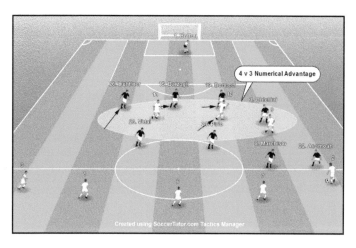

The right wing back Lichtsteiner's reaction can be seen in this diagram.

The white No.10 moves into a more advanced position. Lichtsteiner (the wing back on the weak side) drops back in line with Barzagli (15) and helps create a 4 v 3 numerical advantage at the back for Juventus.

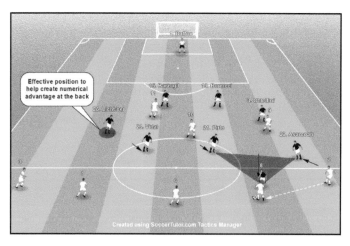

If the white right back (2) passes inside to No.7, Marchisio (8) is the player who puts pressure on him.

The left wing back Asamoah (22) and the defensive midfielder Pirlo (21) create a defensive triangle to block potential through passes.

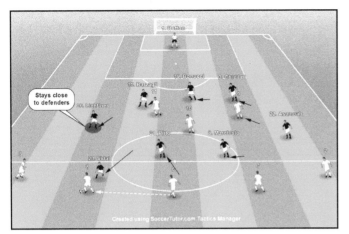

No.7 has passed to No.6 who passes to No.8. As the ball is moving from the left to the right the players continue to shift towards this side, making sure to retain the correct shape.

Lichtsteiner (26), as already mentioned, usually took up a more defensive position compared to the left wing back Asamoah (22). So when the ball gets closer to the right side of Juventus, Lichtsteiner does not move into a more advanced position, but shifts slightly towards the right and stays close to the 3 defenders. This is because Asamoah (22) is in an advanced position.

The ball is passed to the left back (3) and the white No.10 is still in an advanced position. Lichtsteiner (26) has read the tactical situation and as the wing back on the weak side Asamoah (22) is not in an effective position, he stays close to the defenders rather than moving forward to close the man in possession down. This is a job that Vidal (23) has to do.

However, as No.3 has plenty of free space in front of him before Vidal closes him down, an open ball situation is created. The defenders drop back to prevent the forwards from receiving a pass in behind and give time to Vidal to close the ball carrier down.

SESSION FOR THIS TACTICAL SITUATION (2 Practices)

1. Defensive Reactions to Retain a Numerical Superiority When Closing Down the Full Back Against the 4-3-1-2 (1)

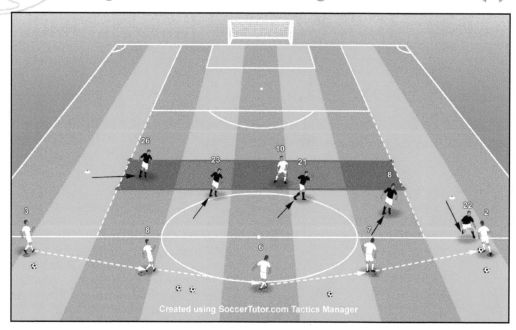

Created using SoccerTutor.com Tactics Manager

Objective

We work with the midfielders on their movements to prevent a numerical equality being created at the back and improve their synchronisation when defending against the 4-3-1-2 formation.

Description

This is a variation of the practices in the previous 4-4-2 and 4-2-3-1 sections and players must coach their teammates to take the correct actions. The white No.10 is inside the blue zone (5 x 44 yards) at all times. The left wing back (22) is in an advanced position on the yellow cone and the right wing back (26) is in a deeper position.

The white players pass the ball to each other while the defending players (black) shift according to the position of the ball. When the ball reaches the white right back (2), the black left wing back (22) always puts pressure on the ball. When the ball reaches the left back (3), the black right wing back (26) or the attacking midfielder (21) puts pressure on him according to the tactical situation.

The defending team need to compensate for the equality in numbers due to the advanced position of No.10, so make the following movements to simulate supporting the defence in different situations:

1. In diagram 1 the right wing back (26) moves inside the blue zone.

2. In diagram 2 the left wing back (22) has moved back into the blue zone so the right wing back (26) can move into an advanced position to put pressure on the ball carrier (3).

3. In diagram 3 the left wing back (22) is in an advanced position so the right wing back (26) stays in a deep position and the midfielder (23) puts pressure on the ball carrier.

PROGRESSION

2. Defensive Reactions to Retain a Numerical Superiority When Closing Down the Full Back Against the 4-3-1-2 (2)

Description

This is a progression of the previous practice. We add 3 black defenders and 2 white forwards who are all positioned inside the blue zone.

The white players pass the ball to each other and when they feel it's the right moment they pass to one of the forwards (9 or 10). The white No.10 moves freely inside both the blue and red zones.

The white team aim to dribble the ball through the red end line or receive a pass inside the yellow zone. The offside rule is applied throughout. The defending team try to win the ball, make a clearance towards the white midfielders and then quickly step up together.

The defending team's wing backs (black 22 and 26) enter the zones when they feel it is the right time to do so. The right wing back (26) is the key in this practice as he has to evaluate the tactical situation and take the appropriate reaction.

In diagram 1 the right wing back (26) enters the red zone to drop in line with the white No.10 and help to create a 4 v 3 situation at the back. If a white forward receives successfully, he drops further back into the blue zone as shown in the diagram.

In diagram 2, the black centre back (15) moves to aggressively mark white No.11, so the right wing back enters the blue zone to cover No.15's position and maintain a 4 v 3 numerical advantage at the back again.

If the right wing back (26) makes a bad judgment his teammates in the blue zone will have to defend in a 3 v 3 situation which would be dangerous.

Restriction

The black centre midfielders (23, 21 and 8) take up the appropriate positions but they don't try to block the through passes.

Progression

A goalkeeper is added to the defending team and the whites aim to score unopposed after dribbling the ball through the end line or after receiving a pass inside the yellow zone.

Coaching Points

1. The defending team must take up the appropriate positions according to the position of the ball.

2. The right wing back (26) needs to use good tactical awareness and drop back at the right moment.

3. It is the responsibility of all the players to retain the correct shape and compactness throughout.

4. The movements of the black defenders and midfielders should be synchronised.

DEFENDING WITH THE REAR BLOCK AGAINST THE 4-3-3

DEFENDING WITH THE REAR BLOCK AGAINST THE 4-3-3

When the rear block played against the 4-3-3 formation there were some adjustments that the team made in order to retain a numerical advantage at the back. This depended on which player put pressure on the opposing full back and which midfielder was in the most advanced position.

Defending With the Rear Block Against the 4-3-3 Formation (1)

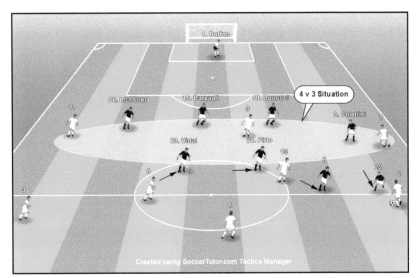

The white right back (2) is in possession. The Juventus left wing back Asamoah (22) is the player who puts pressure on the ball.

There is a 4 v 3 situation at the back because the white No.10 is in a deep position in front of Pirlo (21).

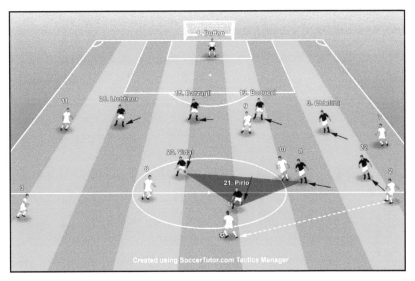

The white No.6 receives the inside pass from No.2. Pirlo (21) moves to close him down immediately and Marchisio (8) together with Vidal (23) creates a defensive triangle to block any potential through passes.

The Juve defenders shift slightly towards the right and the 4 v 3 situation at the back is retained.

Coaching the Juventus 3-5-2: Defending

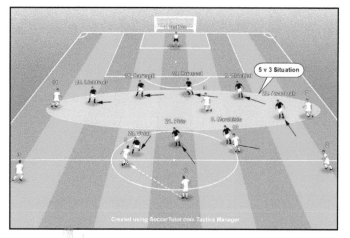

No.6 passes to No.8 and Vidal (23) puts pressure on him. The Juve defenders all shift towards the right.

As the left wing back Asamoah (22) drops back, the situation becomes 5 v 3 at the back.

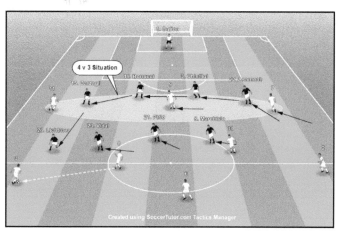

The pass is played to No.3 and the right wing back Lichtsteiner (26) moves forwards to close him down.

The rest of the Juve defenders shift in the form of a chain reaction to the right and Juventus retain a 4 v 3 situation at the back.

The short distances between the players when moving together ensures the effective switching of the opponents' marking.

Defending With the Rear Block Against the 4-3-3 Formation (2)

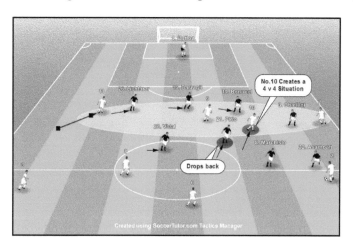

In this situation, the white No.10 moves into an advanced position.

The defence shifts to the left including the wing back on the weak side (Lichtsteiner).

Pirlo (21) drops a few yards deeper to provide support and balance for the defence and compensate for the equality in numbers (4 v 4) at the back.

Coaching the Juventus 3-5-2: Defending

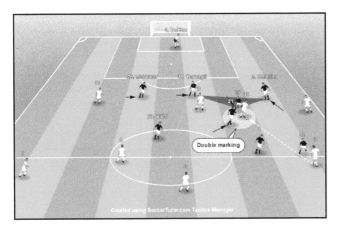

The white No.2 manages to pass forwards to No.10.

Bonucci (19), the closest defender to the white No.10, puts pressure on the ball and Pirlo's (21) deep position enables him to help double mark the ball carrier immediately.

Defending With the Rear Block Against the 4-3-3 Formation (3)

In this situation the ball is passed to No.6. The Juventus midfielders do not move to close him down immediately, but instead shift across to the right.

If Vidal (23) decided to move forwards to close No.6 down the midfield line would become unbalanced as No.8 would be free of marking and would have plenty of space to attack. This reaction gives time to the left wing back Asamoah (22) to drop back and take up a position close to the defenders.

As there is an open ball situation, the Juventus defenders drop back to retain a safe distance from the player in possession.

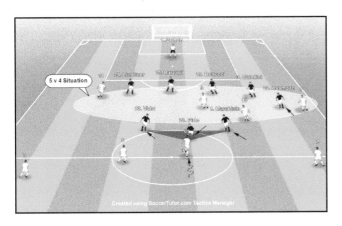

The defenders stop their backward movement just outside of the penalty area. Asamoah (22) is in an effective position and helps create a 5 v 4 situation at the back.

As the white No.6 has moved into an advanced position, Pirlo (21) moves to close him down while Marchisio (8) and Vidal (23) create a defensive triangle to block potential through passes.

The block is balanced and well organised again, with a spare man at the back.

Coaching the Juventus 3-5-2: Defending

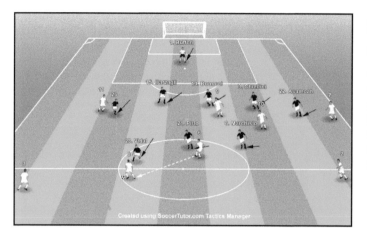

As the Juventus defence is well balanced and compact, the white No.6 passes back to No.8.

Vidal (23) moves to close down the new ball carrier. The Juventus defenders take advantage of the transmission phase (the time the ball takes to travel) and move forwards towards the right, making the block compact again at the same time.

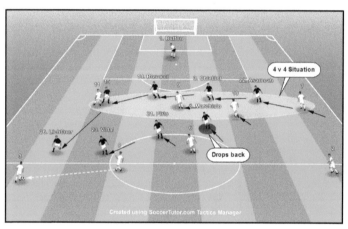

No.8 passes the ball out wide to the left back (3). The right wing back Lichtsteiner (26) moves forwards to put him under pressure, while the rest of the Juve defenders shift towards the right in the form of a chain reaction.

Marchisio (8) sees that Lichtsteiner (26) is the player who puts pressure on the ball and the white No.10 is in an advanced position. This creates a potential 4 v 4 situation at the back for Juve, so Marchisio drops back to be close to the defenders and compensate for this.

Defending With the Rear Block Against the 4-3-3 Formation (4)

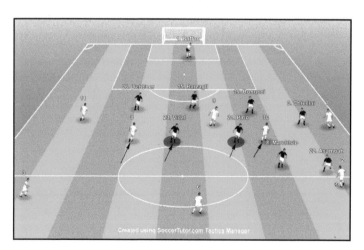

In this final situation the left wing back Asamoah (22) puts pressure on the white right back (2).

Both opposition attacking midfielders (8 and 10) move into more advanced positions, so both Pirlo (21) and Marchisio (8) drop back to get closer to the defence.

SESSION FOR THIS TACTICAL SITUATION (2 Practices)

1. Defensive Reactions to Retain a Numerical Superiority When Closing Down the Full Back Against the 4-3-3 (1)

BLUE CONE:
Att. Mid. Closes

Description

This is a variation of practices in previous sections. The white team have 2 full backs (2 and 3) and 3 midfielders (6, 8 and 10) while the defending team have 3 midfielders (23, 21 and 8) and 2 wing backs (26 and 22).

The 3 white players who are positioned by the red cones start the practice by passing the ball to each other. The 2 white attacking midfielders (8 and 10) move in and out of the blue zone freely. The defending players shift according to the position of the ball and put pressure on the players in possession.

When the ball is passed to one of the white full backs they raise either a yellow or a blue cone. If they raise a yellow cone, the wing back on that side moves to close the player down (diagram 1). If they raise a blue cone, the attacking midfielder on that side moves to close the player down (diagram 3). If the white No.6 has the ball, the black No.21 moves to close him down (diagram 2). The other midfielders provide cover and balance.

The defending players try to retain a numerical advantage inside the blue zone at all times, so if one of the wing backs' moves forward to apply pressure, one of the midfielders must drop back into the zone (diagram 1 - No.8).

Here are the following movements to simulate supporting the defence in different situations:

1. In diagram 1 No.8 is coached to enter the blue zone as the white No.10 moves into it.

2. In diagram 2 all 3 midfielders are outside the blue zone, so both wing backs should be inside.

3. In diagram 3 No.8 puts pressure on the full back, so the midfielders stay out of the blue zone and the wing backs create a 2 v 1 in there.

If both white attacking midfielders (8 and 10) move into the blue zone, the defending team need to create a 3 v 2 situation in there.

PROGRESSION

2. Defensive Reactions to Retain a Numerical Superiority When Closing Down the Full Back Against the 4-3-3 (2)

Description

This is a progression of the previous practice. We add 3 black centre backs (15, 19, and 3) and 3 white forwards (11, 9 and 7) who are all positioned inside the blue zone.

The white players (3, 6 and 2) pass the ball to each other and at the right moment they pass to one of the forwards. The white team aim to dribble the ball through the red end line or receive a pass inside the yellow end zone. The black defending team try to win the ball, make a clearance and then quickly step up together.

The white attacking midfielders (8 and 10) move freely across all zones and try to move into the red zone to create equality in numbers (4 v 4) in attack. The black midfielders try to stop this with one of them dropping back into the red zone to support the defence (No.8 in the diagram example). The offside rule is applied throughout.

Progression: A goalkeeper is added to the defending team and the whites aim to score unopposed after dribbling the ball through the end line or after receiving a pass inside the yellow zone.

Restrictions

1. The black midfielders take up the appropriate positions but they don't try to block the through passes.

2. Once a white forward receives the first pass, no more white players are allowed into the red or blue zone.

3. The defending team's players are not allowed beyond the red end line.

Coaching the Juventus 3-5-2: Defending

CHAPTER 4
FORWARDS' DEFENSIVE POSITIONING

DEFENDING AGAINST A 3 MAN DEFENCE

Defending in a Passive Way Against a 3 Man Defence

If the Juventus forwards' aim was to defend in a passive way within the middle third they had to make sure that they would take up the appropriate positions in order to block the through passes and secure the centre of the pitch. They also tried to stay compact and close to the midfielders.

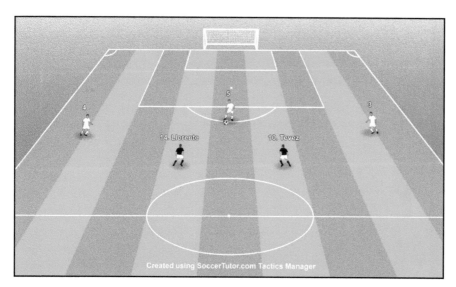

The two Juventus forwards (Llorente and Tevez) take up defensive positions against the opposition's three man defence.

The ball is in the middle centre back's (5) possession.

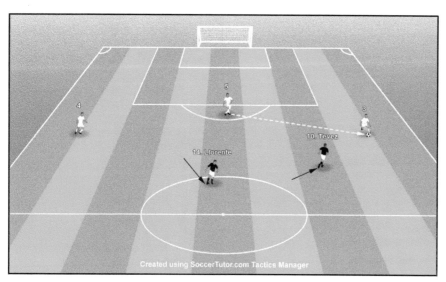

When the defender in possession was near the sideline (No.3 in diagram), one of the forwards (Tevez in diagram) moved towards the strong side while the other forward (Llorente) dropped back towards the centre.

Pressing Against a 3 Man Defence

When the team's aim was to apply pressing, the forwards were the players who started it. Their first aim was to create a strong side and force the ball wide in order to make the opposition's attacks move predictable.

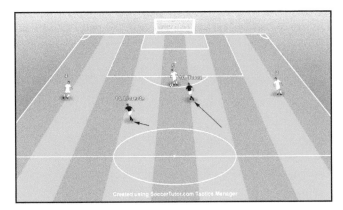

This diagram shows how pressing against a 3 man defence was carried out by Juventus. One forward (Tevez in diagram) moved towards the centre back with the ball in order to put pressure on him and create a strong side (blocking off one side of the pitch). The other forward (Llorente) moved slightly towards the potential strong side.

Llorente had to firstly prevent a forward through pass, so he had to wait until the pass is made before applying pressure on the new ball carrier.

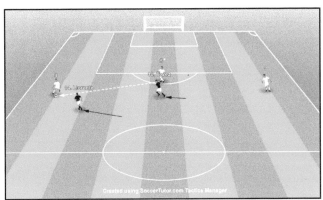

As soon as the ball is passed, Llorente (14) puts pressure on the new man in possession (white No.4), while Tevez (10) prevents No.4 from making an easy back pass to the other centre back No.5.

This movement forces the opposition near the sideline and all of the Juventus players were then able to shift across and create a compact block.

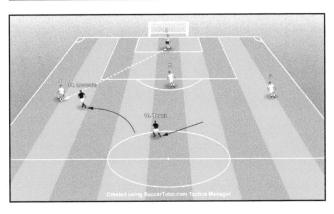

If the pass towards the right or left centre back was made directly from the goalkeeper then Juventus' aim was to press directly after the first pass.

A curved run when putting on pressure (as shown with Llorente in the diagram) could create a strong side. If this was successful, the second striker could then shift immediately towards the strong side rather than moving into an advanced position before moving towards the strong side.

Coaching the Juventus 3-5-2: Defending

Using a Balanced Position Between 2 Players to Force the Ball Wide

If the Juventus forwards' aim was to defend in a passive way within the middle third they had to make sure that they would take up appropriate positions in order to block the through passes and secure the centre of the pitch.

The forwards also tried to stay compact and close to the midfielders. In situations when there was an opposition midfielder in a deep position, the most advanced forward took up a balanced position after the pass to the left or right centre back, in order to control both the defender and the midfielder.

In the diagram above we have added an opposition midfielder (6) to the previous examples. This player would most often be a defensive midfielder who dropped deeper (e.g. in a 3-4-1-2, 3-4-3 or 3-5-2 formation). He takes up a deep position in order to receive the pass towards the centre from the right centre back.

In a situation like this the most advanced forward (Tevez) takes up a balanced position between the centre back (5) and the midfielder (6) in order to control them both.

As the most dangerous pass is the one towards the midfielder (6), the focus should be on the pass towards him in situations when the forward was unable to control both.

Defending in a Passive Way With the Front Block Against a 3 Man Defence

In the diagrams below Juventus had to defend passively within the middle third against a team with 3 players at the back. The players aimed to retain a compact formation with short distances between each other and block the potential through passes towards the centre.

If there was a pass towards a player in the centre, Juventus would immediately put pressure on him by applying double marking, or triple marking if the situation favoured it.

Defending in a Passive Way With the Rear Block Against a 3 Man Defence (1)

In this diagram the pass is directed to the right centre back (4).

The Juventus players shift towards the left and retain short distances between each other. This positioning narrows the passing lanes and the midfielders retain a safe distance from the opponent in possession. This gives them enough time to react to a potential through pass.

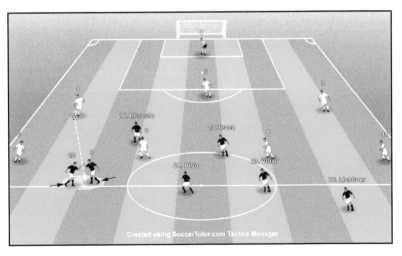

The white No.4 plays a pass forward between Marchisio (8) and Asamoah (22).

Both the narrow passing lane and the safe distance from white No.4 of the two Juventus players enables them to react and intercept the pass.

Coaching the Juventus 3-5-2: Defending

Defending in a Passive Way With the Rear Block Against a 3 Man Defence (2)

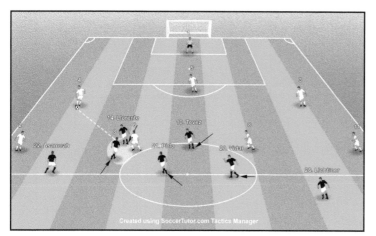

The pass is directed to the white midfielder (6) this time.
The Juventus players react and converge towards the centre.

Llorente (14) and Marchisio (8) block the pass. Pirlo (21) and Tevez (10) move towards the ball zone and get ready to intervene in case the pass is successful.

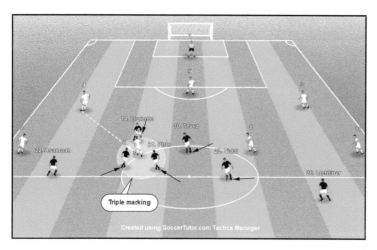

This diagram shows how the Juventus players would react if the pass towards the white No.6 was successful.

As the formation is compact, the distances between the players result in immediate pressure being applied to the new ball carrier by 3 players; Llorente (14), Marchisio (8) and Pirlo (21).

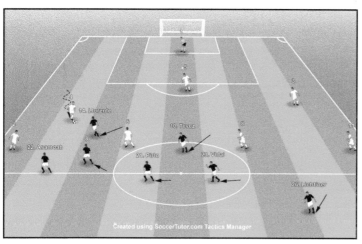

If the white No.4 decides not to pass and moves forward with the ball instead, the Juventus players shift towards the left and Llorente (14) is the first defender.

The Juventus players gather near the ball zone and the formation becomes more compact, so the spaces are squeezed and the passing lanes become narrower.

Defending in a Passive Way With the Rear Block Against a 3 Man Defence (3)

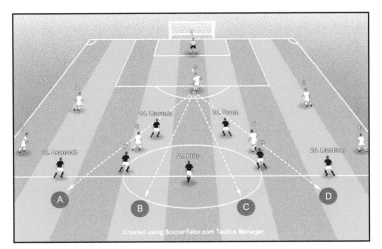

The white centre back (5) has the ball at the edge of the penalty area. The Juventus players aim to retain their compactness and block the potential through passes.

If the white No.5 tries to take up any of the passing options (A, B, C and D in diagram), the Juventus players are ready to block them as the passing lanes are narrow and the safe distance from No.5 allows enough time to react.

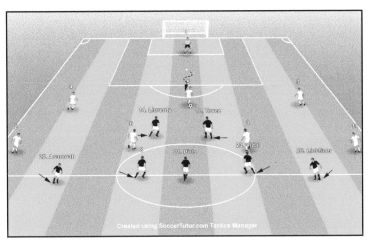

If the white No.5 moves forward with the ball, the Juventus players converge towards the centre and create a compact formation.

The passing lanes become very narrow and it is impossible for the player in possession to achieve successful through passes.

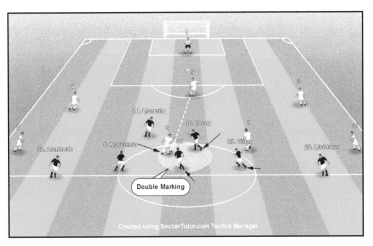

Finally we show what happens if the white No.5 chooses to play a pass instead of moving forward with the ball and the pass is successful.

The pass was successful because the forwards were unable to block it. However, the new man in possession is positioned inside a compact Juventus formation with limited space to exploit, and is immediately under double marking from Tevez (10) and Pirlo (21).

Pressing With the Front Block (Forwards and Midfielders) Against a 3 Man Defence

In the diagrams below it is shown how the Juventus front block (forwards and midfielders) applied pressure against opponents that used a 3 man defence. The main aims for Juventus were:

1. To create a strong side by forcing the ball towards one side of the pitch.

2. After the ball is passed to a player near the sideline, ensure that there is pressure on the new man in possession and the potential receivers of the ball are tightly marked.

3. To create a numerical advantage by moving many players near to the ball zone and applying double marking if possible.

Pressing With the Front Block Against a 3 Man Defence (Starting Positions)

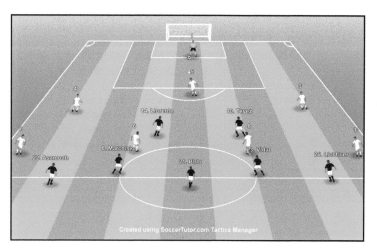

In this diagram we show the starting positions of the forwards and the midfielders in a pressing situation against a 3 man defence which is ideal for Juventus.

The ball is in the goalkeeper's possession.

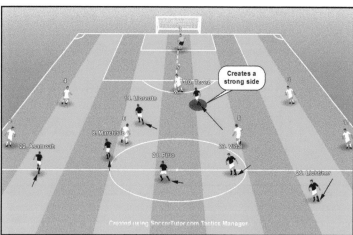

As soon as there is a pass towards the white centre back (5), Tevez moves to put pressure on him and he creates a strong side at the same time, so the ball is forced towards the left side of Juventus. The first aim (shown above) is achieved.

The rest of the Juventus players shift towards the strong side. The wing back on the weak side (Lichtsteiner - No.26) drops into a deeper position so he is ready to provide help to the 3 defenders.

Coaching the Juventus 3-5-2: Defending

Pressing With the Front Block Against a 3 Man Defence
(Putting Pressure on the Ball and Marking the Potential Receivers)

As soon as the white No.5 passes to No.4, Llorente (14) makes a curved run to put pressure on him and prevents the back pass. This action keeps the ball near the sideline and makes play predictable as the man in possession can only pass to No.6 or No.2. Marchisio (8) marks No.6 closely and No.22 Asamoah (together with Marchisio) moves to block the potential through pass and control No.2 who is a potential receiver.

As the curved run of Llorente prevents a pass to No.5, Tevez can drop back and help Juventus create a numerical advantage on the left. If Llorente hadn't blocked the pass to No.5, Tevez would stay close to him and drop back after the pass from No.4 is made.

The 3 Juventus midfielders shift towards the strong side with Pirlo moving close to the ball area to provide help.

Pressing With the Front Block Against a 3 Man Defence
(Double Marking and Creating a Numerical Advantage Near the Ball Zone)

The pass is directed to the right back No.2. Asamoah (22) puts pressure on him and Marchisio (8) times his run to help double mark him. The good synchronisation when shifting across is essential for successful double marking.

Marchisio (8) needs to have an effective position (near the ball zone) and then has to take advantage of the transmission phase in order to be close enough to the player in possession as soon as he receives the ball. With this well timed movement, Marchisio reduces the available time for No.2 to find a solution.

Llorente (14) blocks the pass back and Pirlo (21) shifts towards the left and helps create a numerical advantage around the ball zone. Tevez does the same and gets near to the ball zone creating a 5 v 3 situation, which enables him to mark No.6 if No.2 manages to pass to him. So the third aim is achieved and it is very likely that Juventus will win possession.

By blocking the back pass in the first stage of pressing, Llorente (14) made things easier for his teammates as they all managed to get close to the ball area on time.

Pressing With the Front Block Against a 3 Man Defence
(Variation - **The Attacking Midfielder is Away from the Ball Zone**)

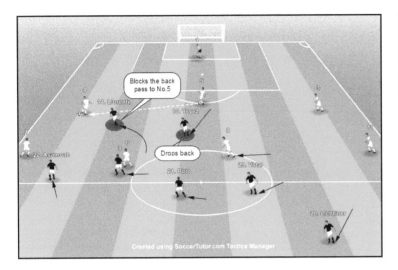

Here we have a similar situation to the previous one but Marchisio (8) hasn't managed to shift towards the left in time as he did in the situation before - he is away from the ball zone.

As soon as the pass is made towards the full back (2) and Asamoah (22) applies pressure, Marchisio (8) judges that the timing is not right to help apply double marking so he stays in a supporting position to Asamoah (22) and close to No.6.

This positioning enables him to block the horizontal pass towards No.6 (option A) and the diagonal pass (option B) as the passing lane between him and Asamoah becomes narrower. The double marking can be carried out with the help of Llorente - this can be done very quickly if the distance between each other is short.

ASSESSMENT:

Applying double marking with the help of the attacking midfielder wasn't always possible. If there wasn't the right timing from the attacking midfielder on the strong side and the man in possession had enough time on the ball and the opportunity to pass the ball to an unmarked teammate towards the centre, the team could be unbalanced and the opposition could easily switch the play.

Blocking the Potential Passes Towards the Centre (1)

If the white No.6 drops into a deeper position, Marchisio (8) does not follow him but stays in a supporting position, otherwise Asamoah (22) would be left without support from the inside and passing option B would be unblocked.

Llorente (14) reads the tactical situation and looks to block the pass towards the white defensive midfielder (6) by dropping into a balanced position between No.4 and No.6 to control both opposing players. The pass towards No.6 is the more dangerous of the two so is Llorente's main focus.

Blocking the Potential Passes Towards the Centre (2)

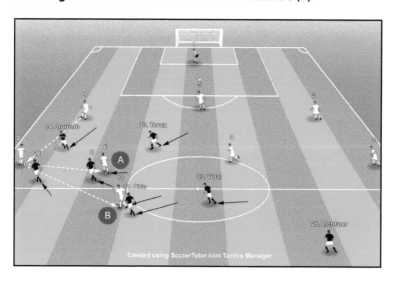

In this diagram there is one more player added for the white team (No.10). This player makes a move to provide a passing option towards the centre as the ball reaches the right back (2).

Despite the fact that Marchisio (8) and Asamoah (22) made the passing lane (B) towards No.10 very narrow, Pirlo (21) follows his movement just in case. The double marking of No.2 is carried out by Asamoah (22) and the forward Llorente (14).

Coaching the Juventus 3-5-2: Defending

Marking the Defensive Midfielder Dropping Back to Receive From the Centre Back

Moves to a balanced positon to mark both No.5 and No.6

Llorente (14) puts pressure on the ball but he doesn't block the back pass. Asamoah (22) and Marchisio (8) shift towards the strong side despite the fact that the white defensive midfielder (6) drops deeper to provide a potential passing option towards the centre.

Tevez is the one who should take over the responsibility of marking No.6. To be able to control both the back pass to No.5 and the pass towards No.6, Tevez takes up a balanced position between the two. However, the most dangerous pass is the one to No.6 so blocking a pass to him is the priority.

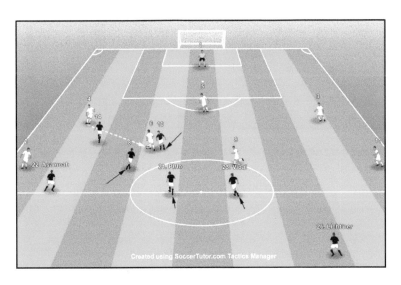

The pass is directed towards the white defensive midfielder (6). Tevez (10) drops back to put pressure on him while Marchisio (8) moves forward to put pressure on him if he manages to turn towards Juventus' goal

The other midfielders also move close to the white No.6 to keep a compact formation. The only option for No.6 is a back pass.

SESSION FOR THIS TACTICAL SITUATION (5 Practices)

1. Defensive Positioning of the Forwards to Block Passes into Midfield

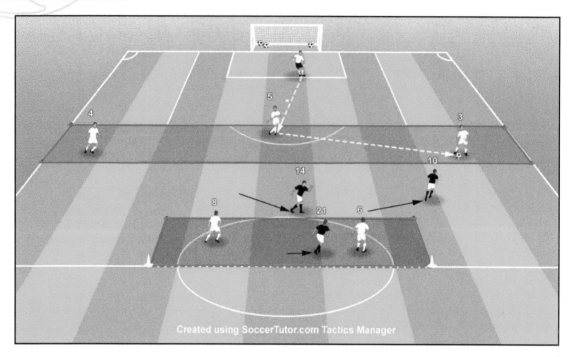

Created using SoccerTutor.com Tactics Manager

Objective

The forwards practice defending in a passive way with the aim of blocking passes into midfield.

Description

We mark out a blue zone (10 x 50 yards) and the 3 white defenders pass the ball to each other after receiving from the goalkeeper. Their aim is to pass to the 2 white centre midfielders inside the red zone (10 x 35 yards).

The 2 white centre midfielders (6 and 8) aim to receive a pass and dribble the ball through the red end line to score (either after a combination play with their teammate or by beating an opponent in a 1 v 1 duel).

The black forwards (14 and 10) try to stay close to the defensive midfielder No.21 (compactness), retain the correct shape in order to block the passes and help the defensive midfielder in case there is a successful pass. If they win possession they counter attack and must score within 6-8 seconds in a 3 v 3 situation (the defensive midfielder takes part in the attack but the white No.8 and No.6 cannot).

Coaching Points

1. The forwards need to take up the appropriate positions according to the position of the ball.

2. The forwards need to have synchronised movements i.e. when one moves to put pressure on the ball carrier, the other drops off into a covering position which provides balance and compactness.

VARIATION

2. Pressing Against a 3 Man Defence and Forcing the Ball Wide in a Zonal Practice

Att. Mid (23) can enter after the ball is in the blue zone for 4 seconds

Objective

We practice pressing against a 3 man defence high up the pitch.

Description

The 2 black forwards (14 and 10) are positioned on the yellow cones inside the middle red zone. The 3 white defenders (4, 5 and 3) start inside 3 separate zones but they are free to move across all zones. The goalkeeper starts with the ball and can pass to any of the 3 centre backs.

The white team's aim is to dribble the ball through the red end line to score. The side defenders (4 and 3) can use diagonal runs into the red zone to receive a through pass and then dribble across the line.

The black forwards try to force the ball wide into the blue zones. If they succeed and the defender with the ball stays inside a blue side zone for more than 4 seconds, the attacking midfielder on the strong side (No.23) enters the zone and helps to double mark the ball carrier.

If the black team win the ball they then counter attack and try to score within 6 seconds in a 3 v 3 situation.

Coaching Point

The forward who closes down the ball carrier should prevent the defender from being able to pass back across the pitch. This forces the ball wide so the black team can block potential passes, press the ball and win it.

PROGRESSION

3. Pressing Against a 3 Man Defence and Forcing the Ball Wide in a Zonal Practice (2)

Att. Mid (23) can enter after the ball is in the blue zone for 4 seconds

Created using SoccerTutor.com Tactics Manager

Objective

We practice pressing against a 3 man defence (+ a defensive midfielder) high up the pitch.

Description

In this progression of the previous practice we add a white defensive midfielder (No.6) who starts by the red cone. This defensive midfielder (6) enters the red zone as soon as the centre back (or goalkeeper) makes a pass towards the left or right centre back.

The forward in the most advanced position (No.14 in the diagram) should evaluate the situation then take the appropriate reaction. The aim for the white team stays the same as in the previous practice (dribble the ball across the red line), but they now also have the option to pass to the defensive midfielder in order to achieve it.

The forwards try to force the ball wide, press the ball to win it and then launch a counter attack to try and score within 6 seconds.

Coaching Points

1. The main aim remains to force the ball wide.

2. Synchronised movements are very important for the forwards. If one forward moves to close down the ball carrier, the other forward must move into the correct position to block potential passing options.

PROGRESSION

4. Pressing With the Front Block and Preventing the Switch of Play in a Dynamic 7 v 7 Game

Created using SoccerTutor.com Tactics Manager

Description

We divide half a pitch in two which helps the players recognise the strong side. The defending team play against the whites who use a 3-4 formation (relates to the 3-4-1-2 or 3-4-3) and they apply pressing. If a centre midfielder is added for the whites their formation becomes a 3-5 (3-5-2 formation). The defending players take up starting positions on the yellow cones. As soon as the white goalkeeper passes the ball, the white team have 3 aims:

1. To complete 5 consecutive passes (1 point).

2. To dribble the ball through the halfway line (1 point).

3. To switch play successfully into one of the 8 x 8 yard boxes on the weak side (1 point).

The whites can score more than 1 point during the same attacking move. The defending team aim to stop the whites scoring points, win the ball and then score within 6-8 seconds (1 point). If the black team lose possession to the white team during their counter attack or the ball goes out of play, the game starts again with the white team's goalkeeper in possession.

Restrictions

1. The white players are not allowed to pass into the penalty area to switch the play towards the weak side.

2. A switch of play is only successful if the pass is received within one of the 8 x 8 yard boxes on the other side. These boxes are not in use in the first phase when the goalkeeper passes the ball out.

Coaching Points

1.   The aim for the black defending team is to create a strong side and force the ball towards the sideline.

2.   Aggressive marking of the potential receivers is needed to prevent the opposition from switching play.

3.   Make sure the players utilise double marking where possible and keep a compact formation at all times.

PROGRESSION

5. Defending Passively Against a 3 Man Defence and Blocking Through Passes in a Zonal Practice

Created using SoccerTutor.com Tactics Manager

Objective

The players practice defending in a passive way against a 3 man defence and blocking passes through the centre.

Description

Using 2/3 of a full pitch we mark out a blue zone (25 yards x full width) and a red zone (15 x 44 yards). The white team have 3 defenders and 4 midfielders in the blue zone and 2 forwards in the red zone. The black team have 2 wing backs, 3 midfielders and 2 forwards all in the blue zone.

The practice starts with the white team's goalkeeper who passes to one of the centre backs.

The defending team (black) wait in the middle third (blue zone). The white team try to score by either making a successful pass to the forwards (7 and 9) inside the red zone or by dribbling the ball through the yellow cones.

In addition, one point is scored every time the whites manage to complete more than 2-3 consecutive passes within the blue zone (depending on the age/level of the players).

Coaching the Juventus 3-5-2: Defending

The defending team aim to defend by waiting for the white players to enter the blue zone and prevent them from achieving each one of their aims. If they win possession, they try to score within 6-8 seconds.

If the black team lose possession to the white team during their counter attack or the ball goes out of play, the game starts again with the white team's goalkeeper in possession again.

Restrictions

1. The black team are not allowed to move out of the blue zone during the defensive phase.

2. The two white forwards are not allowed to move out of the red zone at any time.

Coaching Points

1.   The black team's players must take up the appropriate positions according to the ball position, use synchronised movements and keep compact to block the potential passing lanes towards the forwards

2. The focus in this practice is on defending passively in a certain zone of the pitch and not on the negative transition. This is why if the black team lose the ball after winning it, the practice starts again from the beginning.

3. In the situation described the white team's players are playing with a 3-4-1-2 formation which is easily adapted to a 3-4-3 or 3-5-2.

DEFENDING AGAINST A 4 MAN DEFENCE

Defending in a Passive Way Against a 4 Man Defence

Defending Against a 4 Man Defence

When the team faced a 4 man defence the choice could be either to apply pressing high up the pitch or defend in a passive way by waiting for the opponents to come into a certain zone (mainly in the middle third).

Defending in a Passive Way Against a 4 Man Defence

When the team's aim was to wait for the opponents to come into a certain zone and then apply pressure, the forwards worked in collaboration to prevent the through passes towards the opposition's midfielders, securing the centre of the pitch and keeping a compact formation by staying close to the midfielders.

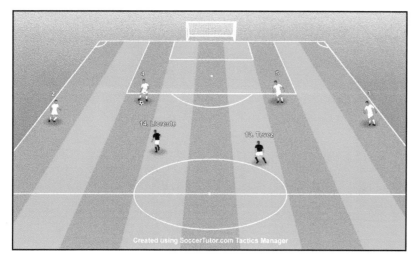

If the ball was in the centre back's possession the 2 forwards took up the positions shown with the weak side's forward (Tevez in the diagram) being in a slightly deeper position.

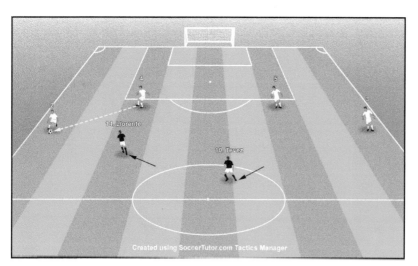

When the ball was in the full back's possession, the two forwards shifted towards the strong side.

The weak side's forward was in a deeper position (Tevez in the diagram).

Coaching the Juventus 3-5-2: Defending

Defending in a Passive Way With the Front Block Against a 4 Man Defence

In these diagrams below Juventus had to defend passively within the middle third against a team with four defenders. The players aim to retain a compact formation, block the potential through passes and double mark the players who manage to receive inside their compact formation.

Defending in a Passive Way With the Rear Block Against a 4 Man Defence

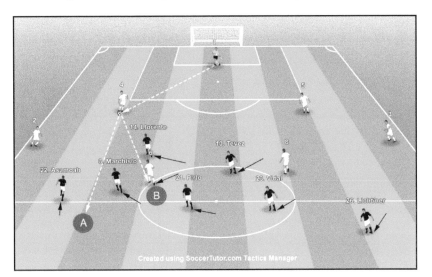

In this diagram the white centre back (4) receives the pass from the goalkeeper.

The Juventus players shift towards the left in order to block the two passing options (A and B) by narrowing the passing lanes.

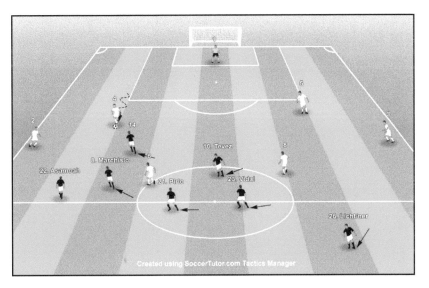

The white No.4 moves forward with the ball.

The team gets more compact, as the man in possession approaches and the distance between him and the defending players is reduced (the less time to react the more compact they should be).

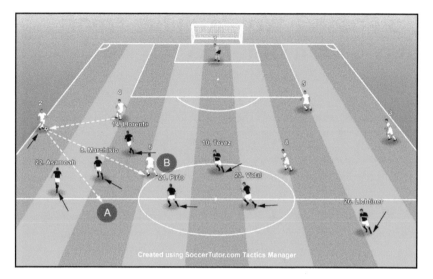

The pass is directed to the white right back (2) who drops a few yards back to receive.

The Juventus players all shift across to the left again. The two passing options (A and B) towards potential players inside Juve's compact formation should be blocked.

If the passes are successful, the new player in possession should be immediately double or triple marked.

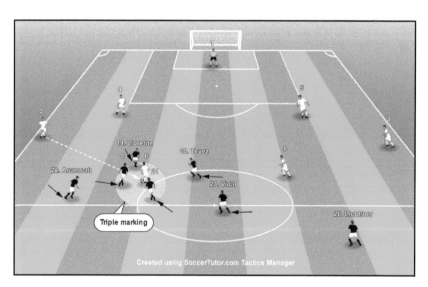

Here we show what happens if the pass inside to white No.6 is successful. As Juventus are in a compact formation 3 players move to mark him; Llorente (14), Marchisio (8) and Pirlo (21).

SESSION FOR THIS TACTICAL SITUATION (2 Practices)

1. Defending Passively Against a 4 Man Defence to Block Passes into Midfield (3 v 6)

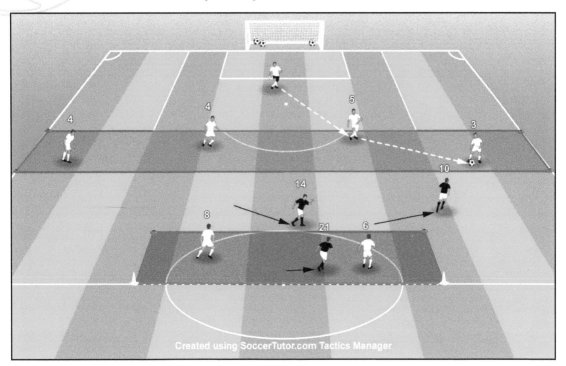

Created using SoccerTutor.com Tactics Manager

Objective

We practice defending in a passive way with the aim of blocking through passes into midfield.

Description

The goalkeeper starts the practice by passing to one of the 4 white defenders inside the blue zone (10 yards x width of pitch). They pass the ball to each other waiting for the right time to pass towards the 2 white midfielders inside the red zone (10 x 35 yards).

The 2 white midfielders (6 and 8) try to receive within the red zone and dribble the ball through the red end line to score (either after a combination play with their teammate or by beating an opponent in a 1 v 1 duel).

We have 1 black defensive midfielder (21) inside the red zone and 2 forwards outside of it. The black forwards (14 and 10) try to stay close to the defensive midfielder (compactness) and retain the correct shape in order to block the through passes.

If the black team are able to win the ball, they should then attack and try to score within 6-8 seconds (3 v 4 situation as the defensive midfielder also takes part in the attack).

PROGRESSION

2. Defending Passively Against a 4 Man Defence to Block Passes into Midfield (7 v 9)

Created using SoccerTutor.com Tactics Manager

Description

Using 2/3 of a full pitch we mark out a blue zone (25 yards x full width) and a red zone (15 x 44 yards). The white team have 4 defenders, 3 midfielders in the blue zone and 2 forwards in the red zone. The black team have 2 wing backs, 3 midfielders and 2 forwards all in the blue zone.

The practice starts with the white team's goalkeeper who passes to one of the centre backs. The white team try to score by either making a successful pass to the players (7 and 11) inside the red zone or by dribbling the ball through the yellow cones.

One point is also scored every time the whites manage to complete more than 2-3 consecutive passes within the blue zone (depending on the age/level of the players).

The black defending team defend by waiting for the white players to enter the blue zone and prevent them from achieving each one of their aims. If they win possession, they try to score within 6-8 seconds (7 v 7 situation).

If the black team lose possession to the white team during their counter attack or the ball goes out of play, the game starts again with the white team's goalkeeper in possession again.

Restrictions

1. The black team's players are not allowed to move out of the blue zone until they win the ball.

2. The two white players (7 and 11) in the red zone must stay there throughout the practice.

Coaching Points

1. The black team's players must take up the appropriate positions according to the position of the ball, use synchronised movements and keep compact to block the potential passing lanes towards the red zone.

2. The players need to read the tactical situation and use synchronised movements to react.

3. A key aspect is to retain the team's cohesion and a compact formation (small spaces between the players).

Pressing With the Front Block Against a Team Using a 4 Man Defence

In the diagrams to follow there will be an analysis of how Juventus pressed against teams with 4 defenders. Juventus had 3 aims to achieve during the pressing application:

1. To create a strong side by forcing the ball towards one side of the pitch.

2. After the ball is passed to a player near the sideline, Juventus ensured that there was pressure on the new man in possession and the potential receivers of the ball were tightly marked.

3. To create superiority in numbers by moving many players near the ball zone and applying double marking if possible.

When Juventus had to apply pressing against a four man defence, either the wing backs or the attacking midfielders had to move into advanced positions to put pressure on the full back with the ball.

On the left side this depended mainly on the position of the full back (deep or advanced). If he was high up the pitch this was mainly the wing back's job. If he had a deeper position, the attacking midfielder was the player who took over the role of the first defender.

On the right it was the attacking midfielder Vidal (23) who mostly moved forward to put pressure on the full back with the ball, regardless of whether the full back was in a deep or advanced position. This was because the right wing back Lichtsteiner (26) is more defensive minded than Asamoah (22) on the left.

Pressing against a four man defence was difficult because both the wing backs and the attacking midfielders had to travel a long distance to be able to put pressure on the ball. This resulted in the opposition having time on the ball, so creating a numerical advantage around the ball zone was difficult as the second forward would not be close enough. Only the shifting across of the defensive midfielder (Pirlo - No.21) could create superiority in numbers but this could not take place immediately.

Finally, the forward on the strong side and the attacking midfielder were the players who could apply double marking to the opposition full back.

Pressing With the Front Block Against a Four Man Defence - Starting Positions

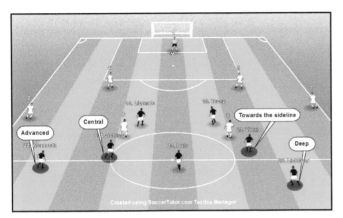

In this diagram we show the starting positions of the forwards and the midfielders with the ball in the goalkeeper's possession.

Lichtsteiner (the right wing back) has a more defensive position than Asamoah (the left wing back) and Vidal (23) is in a slightly wider position than Marchisio (8).

Creating a Strong Side

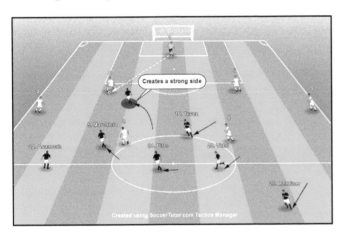

Llorente (14) puts pressure on the centre back (4) using a curved run and creates a strong side.

All the players shift towards the strong side and Lichtsteiner (26) drops back to help create a numerical advantage at the back.

Pressing the Ball and Tightly Marking the Potential Receivers

The ball is passed to the white right back (2). The new man in possession is in a deep position, so Marchisio (8) is the player who puts him under pressure.

Llorente (14) drops back and helps apply double marking as he is close enough to No.2. Marchisio's movement towards the sideline triggers a chain reaction for the midfielders who all shift towards the left.

Pirlo (21) moves into an advanced position and takes over No.6's marking.

    Coaching the Juventus 3-5-2: Defending

Double Marking and Superiority in Numbers Around the Ball Zone

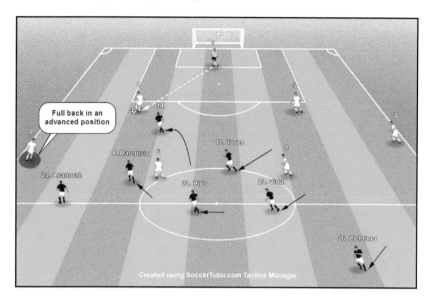

In a similar situation to the previous, the opposition full back (2) is in an advanced position this time.

Llorente (14) creates a strong side while Marchisio (8) is close to No.6 and gets ready to close down the full back (2) if the pass is directed to him.

The centre back passes to No.2, so Asamoah (22) takes advantage of the transmission phase (the time the ball takes to travel) and moves to close him down. Marchisio (8) uses a well timed run to help apply double marking.

Llorente (14) blocks the potential pass back to No.4. Pirlo (21) does not move forward this time but stays deep due to Asamoah's (22) advanced position.

Marchisio blocks the pass to No.6 despite him being close to the ball area, but Tevez still shifts close to him in case there is a successful pass. There is a 4 v 3 situation around the ball zone.

Coaching the Juventus 3-5-2: Defending

Preventing Passes Towards the Centre (1)

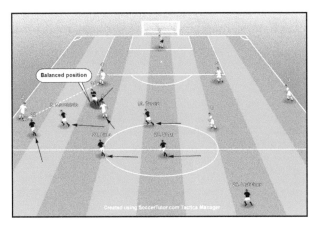

If the opposition's defensive midfielder (6) drops back towards a potential passing lane after No.4's pass, Llorente (14) has to take up a balanced position which enables him to control both the pass to No.4 and the one towards No.6.

The pass towards No.6 is the most dangerous one for Juventus so this is Llorente's priority.

Assessing the Tactical Situation to Decide Whether to Apply Double Marking

In this situation Marchisio (8) judges that the timing isn't right to apply double marking. He chooses to stay in a position where he can support the left wing back Asamoah (22) instead of moving close to the player in possession.

This positioning also enables Marchisio to narrow the passing lane between him and Asamoah (option A), mark No.6 and block the potential inside pass (option B) to him.

Llorente drops back with the aim of retaining a compact formation before applying double marking.

Preventing Passes Towards the Centre (2)

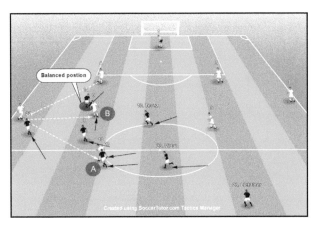

In a similar situation to the previous one, Marchisio (8) doesn't move to double mark the right back (2) and the white No.6 drops into a deeper position to provide a passing option.

Marchisio (8) stays in a supporting position and blocks the potential diagonal pass towards the No.10 (option A) rather than move forward and leave Asamoah (22) without support.

Llorente (14) takes the responsibility of controlling the pass to No.6 (option B) as well as the one to No.4 by dropping into a balanced position between the two of them.

Coaching the Juventus 3-5-2: Defending

Starting the Pressing Application On the Right - Creating a Strong Side

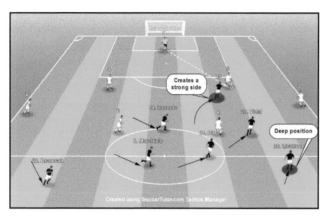

As soon as the pass is played to the white centre back (5) Tevez (10) makes a curved run and creates a strong side.

Vidal (23) shifts towards the right, ready to put pressure on the left back (3) if the pass is directed to him. Pirlo (21) and Marchisio (8) shift across as part of a chain reaction.

On the right side Vidal (23) was usually the player who put pressure on the left back whether he was in a high or deep position. This was because Lichtsteiner (the right wing back) was usually in a deep position.

Pressing the Ball, Double Marking and Tightly Marking the Potential Receivers

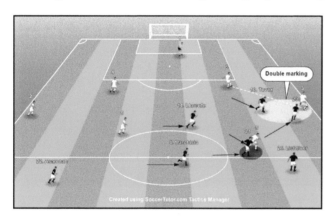

As soon as the pass is directed to the white left back (3) Vidal (23) puts pressure on him and Tevez (10) drops back to help apply double marking.

Pirlo (21) marks the centre midfielder No.8 who moves near the ball area to provide a passing option.

Lichtsteiner (26) stays back and the wing back on the other side (Asamoah) doesn't have to drop too deep.

Preventing the Pass Towards the Centre

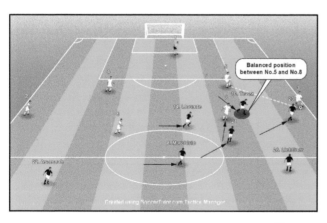

In this situation the white No.8 drops into a deeper position to receive. Marchisio (8) stays in a supporting position to Asamoah again.

The forward Tevez (10) reads the tactical situation and drops into a balanced position between No.8 and No.5, with the main priority to block a pass to No.8.

In this situation Pirlo (21) is in an advanced position as the right wing back Lichtsteiner (26) is in a deep position.

Pressing When the Winger is in a Deep Position On the Strong Side

In situations when there was a winger in a deep position on Juventus' left side and the distances between the defenders were too big to ensure the effective switch in the opponents' marking, the wing back didn't risk moving forward to put pressure on the right back with the ball. Instead he stayed close to his direct opponent and let the attacking midfielder do the job.

Defending When the Winger is in a Deep Position On the Strong Side (No Chain Reaction)

In this example the white team's right midfielder (7) is in a deep position.

Chiellini (3) is too far away from the left wing back Asamoah (22) so a chain reaction (shifting and switching the marking of players) cannot take place.

Chiellini communicates with Asamoah so he does not move forwards.

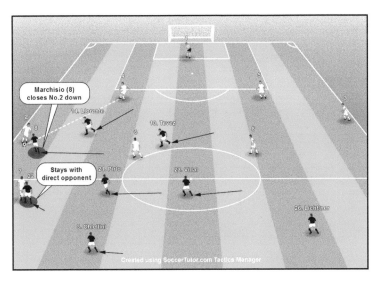

As soon as the pass is directed to the right back (2), Marchisio (8) has either read the tactical situation or been informed by Asamoah, so he takes over the responsibility of closing the new player in possession down.

The left wing back Asamoah (22) stays close to his direct opponent - the right winger No.7.

Defending When the Winger is in a Deep Position On the Strong Side (Chain Reaction)

In this example the distance between the centre back Chiellini (3) and the left wing back Asamoah (22) is much shorter.

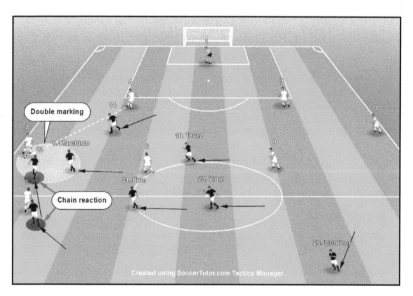

As there is coaching between the players, when the pass is made towards the white right back (2), Asamoah (22) takes advantage of the transmission phase (the time the ball takes to travel) and puts pressure on No.2.

At the same time, in the form of a chain reaction, Chiellini (3) takes over the right winger No.7's marking and Marchisio (8) moves to help apply double marking.

SESSION FOR THIS TACTICAL SITUATION (5 Practices)

1. Synchronised Double Marking On the Left Flank and Blocking Passes Towards the Centre (1)

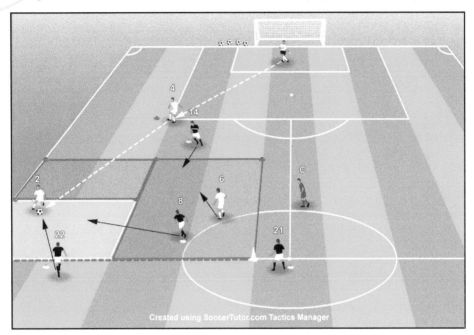

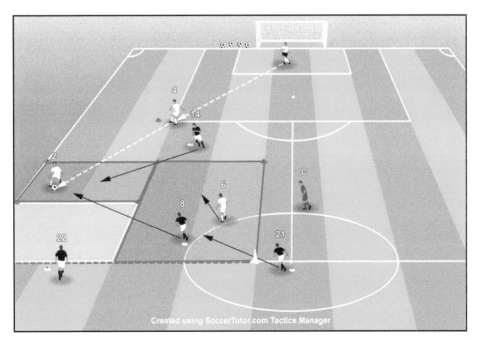

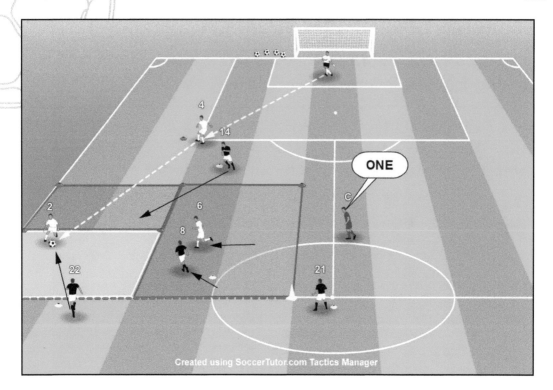

Created using SoccerTutor.com Tactics Manager

Description

Using 1/4 of a full pitch and the penalty area we mark out two 20 x 20 yard zones as shown. The zone next to the sideline is divided in two (red and yellow). The players starting positions are on the yellow cones except for the white No.6 who moves freely inside the blue zone and No.2 who moves freely inside the red and yellow zones.

The whites' aim is to pass the ball to No.6 (1 point) and dribble the ball through the end red line (3 points) while the defending players aim to prevent both. The goalkeeper starts by passing to the centre back (4) and the defending players (black) move accordingly. The forward's (14) role is to force the play towards No.2 and prevent the through pass to No.6. When the pass towards No.2 is made, the defending players move to double mark him.

Which players participate in the double marking depends on the area in which No.2 receives the ball:

- **Diagram 1:** If No.2 receives in the yellow zone, the wing back (22) applies pressure and the attacking midfielder (8) helps to double mark him. The forward (14) moves back in case No.6 drops deep. In this situation the defensive midfielder (21) doesn't take part.

- **Diagram 2:** If the white No.2 receives deeper in the red zone, No.8 is the player who presses him and No.14 helps to double mark. No.21 shifts (as part of a chain reaction) and marks white No.6.

- **Diagram 3:** When No.2 is in the yellow zone and we don't want No.8 to move across, the coach calls a code word "ONE". Only the wing back (22) closes No.2 down. No.8 is in a supporting position and No.14 either drops back to double mark or moves back to prevent No.6 from receiving in a deep position.

Restrictions: 1. White No.2 should use at least two touches. 2. The whites are not allowed to pass back to No.4.

Progression: As soon as the defending players win possession they launch a counter attack and must score within 6-8 seconds using 1/4 of the pitch and the penalty area.

VARIATION

2. Synchronised Double Marking On the Left Flank and Blocking Passes Towards the Centre (2)

Created using SoccerTutor.com Tactics Manager

Description

This practice is a variation of the previous one. One player is added for the whites (No.10) who is inside the white box as shown in the diagram.

This time the defending team (black) have to block the pass towards the No.10 who aims to receive a pass within the white box (3 points). The black team also still have to prevent the whites from dribbling the ball through the red line (3 points) and passing towards No.6 (1 point).

Restrictions

1. White No.2 should use at least two touches.

2. The whites are not allowed to pass back to No.4.

3. The No.10 is not allowed to leave the white box and must receive the pass within it to score 3 points.

Progression

As soon as the defending players win possession they launch a counter attack and must score within 6-8 seconds using 1/4 of the pitch and the penalty area.

VARIATION

3. Synchronised Double Marking On the Right Flank and Blocking Passes Towards the Centre

Created using SoccerTutor.com Tactics Manager

Description

Using 1/4 of a full pitch and the penalty area we mark out two 20 x 20 yard zones as shown in the diagram. The players starting positions are on the cones except for the white No.8 who moves freely inside the blue zone. The whites' aim is to pass the ball to No.8 (1 point) and dribble the ball through the end red line (3 points) while the defending players aim to prevent both.

The goalkeeper starts by passing to the centre back (5) and the defending players (black) move accordingly and the defensive midfielder (21) can enter the blue zone. However, the forward (10) is the one who has to force the play towards the white left back (3) and prevent the through pass towards No.8.

When the pass towards No.3 is made, the black No.10 and the attacking midfielder (23) move to double mark him and try to win the ball while also blocking the pass towards white No.8. The defensive midfielder (21) marks No.8 if he is in an advanced position. If he drops deep then the forward (10) should prevent him from receiving.

Restrictions

1. White No.3 should receive on the red cone and then move with the ball or pass, using at least two touches.

2. The whites are not allowed to pass back to No.5.

Progression: As soon as the defending players win possession they launch a counter attack and must score within 6-8 seconds using 1/4 of the pitch and the penalty area.

VARIATION

4. Pressing On the Left Flank When the Opposition Winger is in a Deep Position

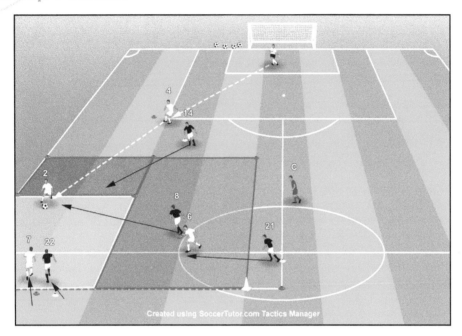

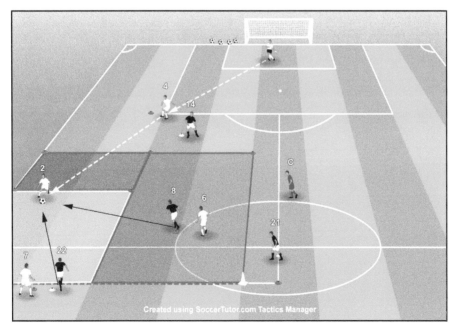

Objective

We practice applying pressing on the left when the opposition winger was in a deep position.

Description

Using a little more than a quarter of a full pitch and the penalty area we mark out two 20 x 25 yard zones as shown in the diagram. The players starting positions are on the cones except for the white No.6 who moves freely inside the blue zone and No.2 who moves freely inside the red and yellow zones.

The whites' aim is to pass the ball to No.6 (1 point) and dribble the ball through the end red line (3 points) while the defending players aim to prevent both.

The goalkeeper starts by passing to the centre back (4) and the defending players (black) move accordingly. The white winger (7) can enter the yellow zone or stay outside of it. The white right back No.2 should receive the pass from his teammate within the yellow zone.

The black team's players' have to recognise the tactical situation and respond in the right way:

- **Diagram 1:** If the white winger (7) enters the yellow zone, the black left wing back (22) marks him and doesn't move forward to put pressure on No.2. The black attacking midfielder (8) should read the situation and shift to close No.2 down. In this example, because the left wing back (22) is in a deep position and double marking is applied with the help of the forward (14), the defensive midfielder (21) enters the blue zone to mark the white No.6.

- **Diagram 2:** If the white winger (7) stays outside, the black wing back (22) can move forward and close down the ball carrier. In this situation the attacking midfielder (8) helps to apply double marking and the black defensive midfielder (21) stays out of the blue zone (the forward No.14 can enter in case No.6 drops back to receive).

Restrictions

1. The white No.2 should use at least two touches.

2. The whites are not allowed to pass back to No.4.

Progression

As soon as the defending players win possession they launch a counter attack and must score within 6-8 seconds using quarter of the pitch and the penalty area.

PROGRESSION

5. Pressing On the Flank With the Opposition Winger in a Deep Position - Functional Practice

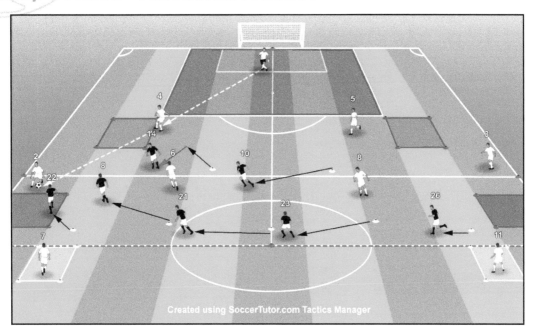

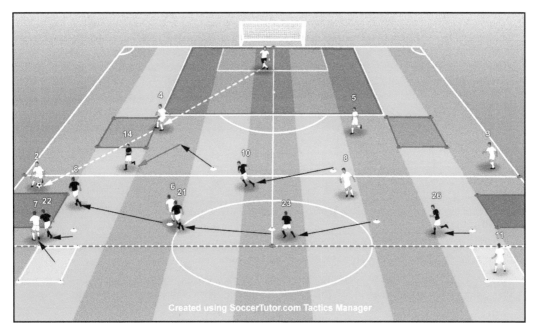

Objective

To apply pressing using the front block against a four man defence.

Description

Using half a full pitch we divide it into 4 sections as shown. This helps the players recognise the strong side as well as helping to indicate the full back's position (high or deep). There are also 4 blue boxes (8 x 8 yards - two on each side) near the sidelines which are the target areas for a potential switch of play and 2 yellow boxes (4 x 4 yards) for the white team's wingers (7 and 11).

The white team play with a 4-2 formation which relates to the 4-4-2 or 4-2-3-1. If a centre midfielder is added the formation becomes 4-1-2 which relates to the 4-3-3 or a 4-3-1-2.

The white team have 3 aims:

1. To complete 5 consecutive passes.

2. To dribble the ball through the halfway line (red).

3. To switch play successfully towards a player within a blue box on the weak side.

The defending team try to prevent these 3 aims from happening. They apply pressing against a team with 4 players at the back, try to win possession and then score within 6-8 seconds (counter attack).

The white winger on the strong side (No.7 in diagram) should enter the playing area (diagram 2) or not (diagram 1) as soon as the goalkeeper makes the first pass.

- **Diagram 1:** If the white winger (7) stays in the yellow box, the black wing back (22) can move forward and close down the ball carrier. In this situation the black defensive midfielder (21) should not move into an advanced position.

- **Diagram 2:** If the white winger (7) enters the playing area, the black wing back (22) marks him and doesn't move forward to put pressure on No.2. The black attacking midfielder (8) should read the situation and shift to close No.2 down. In this example the left wing back (22) is in a deep position so the defensive midfielder (21) moves into an advanced position (not too advanced) to mark the white No.6 as part of a chain reaction.

Restriction

The white players are not allowed to pass back to their goalkeeper or any other teammate inside the penalty area in order to obtain a switch of play towards the weak side.

Coaching Points

1. The focus of this practice is on pressing and not the transition phase. If the black team lose possession while trying to score a goal, the game starts again with the white goalkeeper and the players return to their starting positions.

2. The black team need to use aggressive marking against the potential receivers and should look to utilise double marking whenever possible to try and win possession.

3. The black team need to make sure they retain a compact formation with short distances between each other, using synchronised movements. This enables them to pass on players' marking far more easily.

CHAPTER 5
DEFENDING AGAINST THE 3-4-3

DEFENDING AGAINST THE 3-4-3

On the diagrams to follow there are several situations that show how Juventus defended against the 3-4-3.

The Front Block Defend in a Passive Way Against the 3-4-3

When defending in a passive way, the Juventus players waited within the middle third for their opponents to come. At the same time they tried to retain a compact formation and block the potential through passes. In situations when there was a successful through pass, the new player in possession did not have much space to take advantage of, and he was immediately put under pressure.

Starting Positions

The ball is in the goalkeeper's possession. Against the 3-4-3 there was a 3 v 3 at the back. In order to compensate for the equality in numbers, one of the wing backs (usually Lichtsteiner) moved into a deeper position to create a 4 man defence. Tevez was in a slightly more advanced position than Llorente in order to force the ball towards the left side and Vidal shifted slightly towards the right to be closer to the opposing wing back.

Coaching the Juventus 3-5-2: Defending

Defending in a Passive Way Within the Middle Third Against the 3-4-3 (1)

The aim for Juventus here is to wait for the opponents to come into the middle third. The pass is directed to the left back (3) and all the Juventus players shift towards the right.

The formation is kept compact as the distances between the players remain short, and the players retain a safe distance from the man in possession.

The key element in this situation is that Vidal (23) is the player who moves to close down No.11. The wing back Lichtsteiner (26) stays close to the defenders to retain the 4 v 3 advantage at the back.

Defending in a Passive Way Within the Middle Third Against the 3-4-3 (2)

In this variation, the white centre back (5) chooses to pass directly to the left midfielder (11). The Juventus players all shift towards the right and retain a compact formation.

Vidal (23) puts pressure on the man in possession and Tevez (10) drops back to mark No.8.

The right centre back Barzagli (15) does not follow the No.10 when he drops into a very deep position. He is left under Pirlo's (21) supervision instead.

Defending a Switch Of Play Against the 3-4-3
(The Receiver Doesn't Have Enough Time On the Ball)

In this situation the whites have managed to switch the point of attack successfully from the left side to their right back No.2.

This situation is in favour of Juventus and there is no need to make significant adjustments. There is already a numerical advantage at the back (4 v 3) and the defensive line is well organised and balanced as the right wing back Lichtsteiner (26) didn't have to shift extensively towards the right.

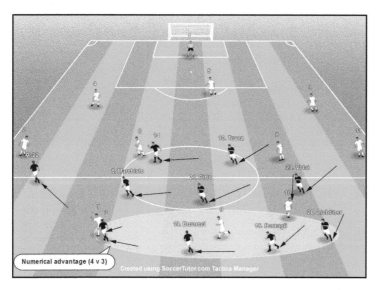

Asamoah's (22) distance from the right back (2) is already short and he takes advantage of the transmission phase (the time the ball takes to travel) to close him down quickly.

Chiellini (3) moves across and marks his direct opponent No.7 as the distance from him was already short. As Marchisio (8) is a few yards away from being in a supporting position, Asamoah (22) is coached to force No.2 towards the sideline in order to give Marchisio time to take up an effective position.

As the No.2 doesn't have enough time on the ball, the white forwards don't move to receive a pass in behind and the Juve defenders don't have to drop back at all.

The Opposition Attempt to Create Space On the Flank

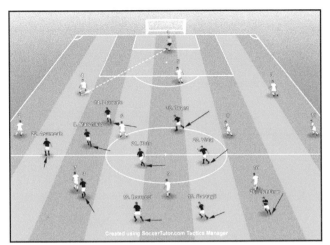

The ball is passed to the centre back (4) from the goalkeeper.

The team's aim in this situation is to wait for the opponents to come and not to apply pressing.

All of the Juventus players shift towards the left, retain a compact formation and narrow the potential passing lanes.

At the back there is a 4 v 3 numerical advantage.

The white right midfielder (2) and the right forward (7) move in opposite directions (synchronised) to create space on the flank.

As the Juventus left wing back Asamoah (22) doesn't have an effective position against his direct opponent, if the left centre back Chiellini (3) follows No.7's movement, it is very likely that the white No.2 could receive a long pass into the created space.

Chiellini reads the tactical situation and drops back rather than following No.7.

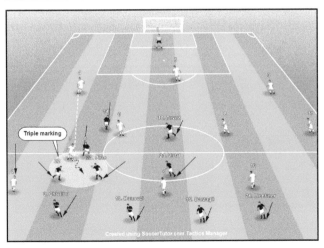

The white centre back (4) doesn't play the long pass to No.2 because Chiellini takes up a good position and the whole back four drop back.

The ball is passed to the right forward (7) and 3 Juventus players move to triple mark the new man in possession.

Pressing Against the 3-4-3

When pressing Juventus' aim was to force the ball towards one side in order to create a strong side and then put pressure on the ball. At the same time they mark all potential receivers and (if possible) create a numerical advantage near the ball zone.

Contesting the Receiver Aggressively After a Long Pass

In this example the aim is to press as soon as the first pass is played.

Tevez (10) moves to put pressure on the ball and creates a strong side, forcing the play to Juventus' left side.

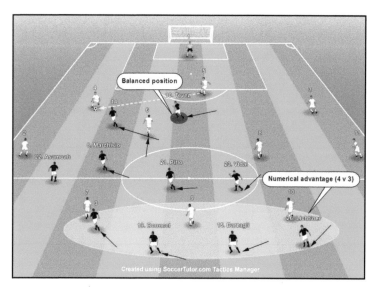

The ball is passed to No.4 and Llorente (14) puts pressure on him.

As No.6 drops into a deeper position, Tevez has to control both him and No.5.

The rest of the Juventus players shift towards the left and there is a numerical advantage (4 v 3) at the back.

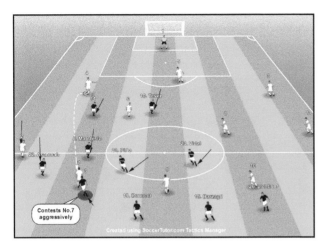

As the passing lanes for through passes are narrow, the white centre back (4) decides to play a long pass towards the right forward (7). Chiellini (3) should aggressively contest him as the situation favours it. If he can't reach the ball first, he tries to force his opponent to lose control of the ball.

At the same time, Pirlo (21) moves from the inside to help double mark No.7 and Marchisio (8) moves near the ball zone too, ready to win the ball if the opponent makes a mistake. Asamoah (22) drops back to prevent a through pass towards No.2 who makes a forward movement.

Defending a Switch Of Play Against the 3-4-3 (Receiver Has Time On the Ball)

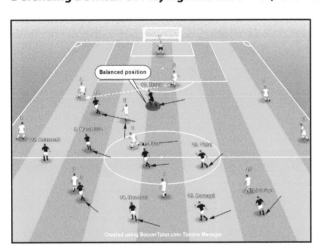

In this situation Juventus look to apply pressing on the left. Tevez is in a balanced position between No.5 and No.6.

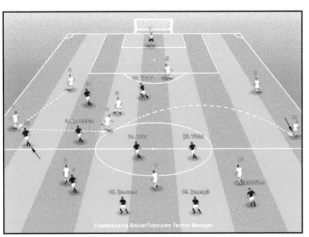

The opposition find a way to switch the point of attack. As the left wing back Asamoah (22) had shifted near to the sideline all of the Juventus players had moved towards the left.

After the switch of play from the opposition, the new man in possession (11) has enough time on the ball as the closest Juventus player is too far away to close him down.

Coaching the Juventus 3-5-2: Defending

The left midfielder (11) moves forward with the ball. The right wing back Lichtsteiner (26) must decide whether it is the right time to press. There is an open ball situation and the white forwards (7, 9 and 10) move to receive in behind. All the Juventus defenders move back and shift towards the right in order to prevent this from happening.

There is a 4 v 3 situation at the back but if Lichtsteiner closes No.11 down it will be 3 v 3. Barzagli (15) should move across to mark No.10, which forces Lichtsteiner to play for time instead of moving forward.

As the left wing back Asamoah (22) is in an advanced position it is best for Lichtsteiner to wait for the midfielders to drop into effective positions and create a compact formation with the defenders. The midfielders move closer to the defenders and are capable of compensating for the equality in numbers and provide support to the wing back (Vidal supports Lichtsteiner).

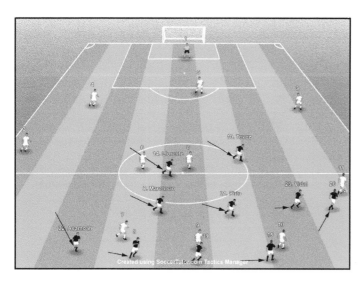

As the midfielders have created a compact formation together with the defenders and Barzagli has taken over No.10's marking, Lichtsteiner (26) moves to close No.11 down with Vidal (23) in a supporting position.

The wing back on the weak side Asamoah (22) is also in an effective defensive position.

As soon as Lichtsteiner (26) forces No.11 to shield the ball, a closed ball situation arises, so the defenders stop their backward movement.

The players are in their appropriate positions and the team has good shape, compactness and organisation.

Coaching the Juventus 3-5-2: Defending

All Potential Receivers are Tightly Marked When Pressing Against the 3-4-3

The ball is directed from the goalkeeper towards the left centre back (3). Tevez (10) moves to put pressure on him and forces the ball wide. As the pass towards white No.5 is blocked, Llorente (14) moves towards the right. The other players also move towards the strong side.

The right wing back Lichtsteiner (22) does not move forward to close down the left midfielder (11) as Juve's left wing back Asamoah (22) is in an advanced position and is unable to drop back immediately and help create a numerical advantage at the back.

Lichtsteiner stays close to the other defenders to help retain the 4 v 3 situation.

As the ball is played to white No.11, Vidal (23) becomes the first player to put pressure on him. Tevez (10) drops back to apply double marking.

The deep position of Lichtsteiner (26) enables Pirlo (21) to move into a more advanced position and control the white No.8.

Lichtsteiner is coached to take over No.10's marking and all the potential receivers are tightly marked.

The defenders can take advantage of the 4 v 3 situation at the back and contest their direct opponents aggressively (tight marking).

Defending With a 3 v 3 Situation at the Back Against the 3-4-3

In all the situations analysed previously, Juventus retained a balanced formation easily with a good control of the space and with a numerical advantage at the back. The only way for a team using the 3-4-3 system to trouble Juventus was to move one of their midfielders into an advanced position, like the example shown below.

The goalkeeper passes to the left centre back (3) and No.8 makes a diagonal movement behind Vidal (23). This movement would create a 4 v 4 situation at the back as the wing back on the weak side Asamoah (22) isn't in an effective position yet.

Pirlo (21) reads the tactical situation and drops back close to the defenders in order to compensate for the equality in numbers (4 v 4).

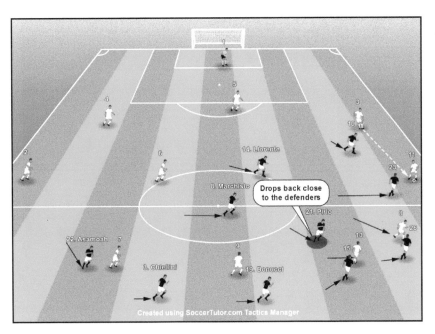

No.3 passes to No.11 and Vidal (23) puts pressure on him. Lichtsteiner (26) takes over No.8's marking.

The rest of the players shift towards the right while Pirlo (21) moves closer to the defenders and Asamoah (22) moves into a deeper position to help create a numerical advantage at the back.

As soon as the pass is directed to No.10, Barzagli (15) moves to contest the new ball carrier and Pirlo (21) moves across to help double mark him. Even if Juventus do not win the ball immediately, time is given to Asamoah (26) to be able to drop back into an effective position.

We now have 5 v 4 situation at the back, so the team is organised and better able to deal with this tactical situation.

SESSION FOR THIS TACTICAL SITUATION (2 Practices)

1. Defending Passively Against the 3-4-3 Using a Compact Formation

Created using SoccerTutor.com Tactics Manager

Objective

We work on defending in a passive way against the 3-4-3 formation in an 11 v 11 game.

Description

Using 2/3 of a full sized pitch we mark out a zone (35 yards x full width) where all the black outfield players are positioned. The goalkeeper starts and passes to one of the 3 defenders who are positioned outside the blue zone.

The defending team (black) stay compact and wait for the opposition to enter the blue zone (representing the middle third). The white team can score in the following ways:

1. Shooting in the goal past the goalkeeper.
2. Completing a set amount of consecutive passes within the blue zone (depending on the age/level of the players).
3. Retaining possession for 4-5 seconds within the blue zone.

Coaching the Juventus 3-5-2: Defending

The black team defend by waiting for the white players to enter the blue zone and then try to prevent them from maintaining possession or scoring.

If the black team win possession, they must try to score in the opposite goal within 6-8 seconds. If the black team lose possession to the whites in their counter attack, the game starts again with the white team's goalkeeper. The focus is on defending passively in a certain zone of the pitch and not on the negative transition.

Coaching Points

1. Players must take up the appropriate positions according to the position of the ball and block the potential vertical or diagonal passing lanes towards the forwards.

2. Synchronised movements are needed to maintain small distances between each other and to retain the team's cohesion. This enables the players to pass on the marking of opponents much more easily.

3. The players need to initially retain a compact formation to defend and then quickly react to any change in the tactical situation.

ASSESSMENT:

This practice can be adjusted for all different formations.

Coaching the Juventus 3-5-2: Defending

PROGRESSION

2. Collective Pressing and Preventing a Switch of Play Against the 3-4-3

Objective

We work on defending by pressing against the 3-4-3 formation in an 11 v 11 game.

Description

Using 2/3 of a full sized pitch we divide the pitch in half vertically, which helps the players recognise the strong side of the pitch and whether the full back's position is high or deep. There are also 4 blue boxes (8 x 8 yards) near the sidelines as shown, which are the target areas for a potential switch of play by the white team.

The practice starts with the goalkeeper and the white team can score in 3 following ways:

1. Shooting in the goal past the goalkeeper.

2. Completing 5 consecutive passes.

3. A successful switch of play from one side to the other with a wide player receiving the pass within one of the blue boxes.

The black team aim to prevent the whites from achieving their 3 aims, win possession and then try to score within 6-8 seconds (counter attack).

If the black team lose possession to the whites in their counter attack, the game starts again with the white team's goalkeeper. The focus is on pressing and not on the negative transition.

Restriction: The white players are not allowed to pass back to the goalkeeper or any other teammate inside the penalty area to try and switch the play towards the weak side of the black team.

Coaching Points

1. The players need to use aggressive marking against the potential receivers.

2. Double marking should be used when possible (good communication is needed).

3. The black team should retain a compact formation with small distances between each other, making sure to make the right movements to cover each other in a chain reaction.

ASSESSMENT:

This practice can be adjusted for all different formations.

CHAPTER 6
DEFENDING AGAINST THE 3-4-1-2

DEFENDING AGAINST THE 3-4-1-2

In the diagrams to follow we show how Juventus defended against teams which used the 3-4-1-2 formation.

Defending in a Passive Way

When defending in a passive way, the Juventus players waited in the middle third for the opposition. At the same time they tried to retain a compact formation and block the potential through passes. If there was a successful through pass, the new player in possession would have limited space and was immediately put under pressure.

Starting Positions

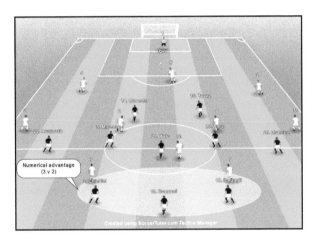

In this diagram we show the starting positions of the Juventus players against the 3-4-1-2 formation.

The team has a spare man at the back with a 3 v 2 numerical advantage. However, the positioning of the white attacking midfielder (10) can change this as shown in the next diagram.

Starting Positions (Advanced Positioning of the Attacking Midfielder)

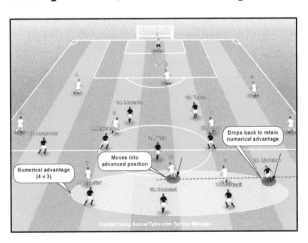

The ball is in the goalkeeper's possession and the white No.10 takes up a more advanced position.

One of the wing backs, usually the most defensive minded (Lichtsteiner - No.26), drops into a position to provide safety. This position is towards the centre and deeper than the white No.10. Lichtsteiner is ready to provide help to his defenders.

Coaching the Juventus 3-5-2: Defending

Starting Positions (The Ball is in the Left Centre Back's Possession)

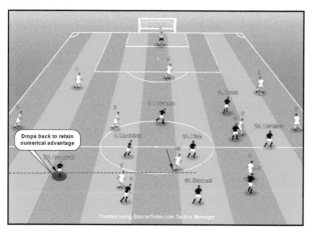

Here again the white No.10 is in an advanced position.

In contrast to the previous example the ball is near the sideline, so the weak side's wing back (Asamoah - No.22 in the diagram) was responsible for restoring the numerical advantage at the back by dropping into a defensive position.

Aggressive Marking of the Forward When Defending Passively

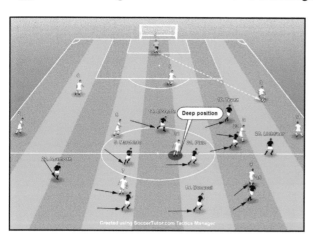

The pass is played from the goalkeeper out wide to the left centre back (3) and the white No.10 is in a deeper position this time.

The Juventus players all shift towards the right and defend passively (not pressing). The passing lanes become narrower and the players gather near the ball zone.

Asamoah (22) drops back to provide more safety at the back, despite the fact that there is already a 3 v 2 situation.

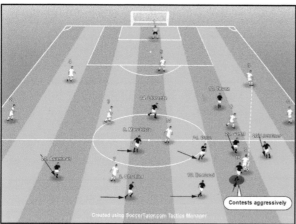

Normally the through pass towards the white forward (9) would not be successful, but in this situation the white centre back (3) manages to find No.9.

Juventus are in a compact formation with short distances between each other. Barzagli (15) is able to contest the new man in possession aggressively as the situation favours it.

Vidal (23) drops back to be near the ball zone and so do Pirlo (21) and Lichtsteiner (26). If the white No.9 has a bad first touch, Juventus will win possession immediately.

Playing for Time to Compensate for Equality in Numbers at the Back

In this example the white forward (9) moves towards the sideline and No.10 moves towards the free space created. As No.10's movement is close to the ball zone and he may be a potential receiver, Pirlo (21) follows him for a few yards.

On the weak side, Asamoah (22) moves back as he is the player who has the responsibility of restoring the numerical advantage in defence. Bonucci (19) moves close to No.10 to control him. Barzagli (15) follows No.9.

As soon as No.3 passes to No.9, Barzagli is coached to play for time until a numerical advantage is restored at the back (4 v 3).

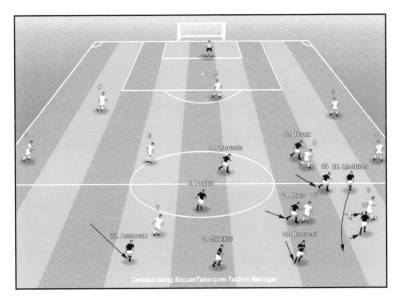

The white forward (9) holds the ball under Barzagli's pressure. Barzagli (15) plays for time until either Asamoah or Lichtsteiner drops back into an effective position and a numerical advantage is restored at the back (4 v 3). Once this is achieved, Barzagli can switch to be more aggressive and try to win the ball.

In this example coaching between the players is needed to control the situation.

Coaching the Juventus 3-5-2: Defending

Pressing Against the 3-4-1-2

During the pressing application Juventus aimed to force the ball towards one side in order to create a strong side and then put pressure on the ball. At the same time they mark all the potential receivers and (if possible) create a numerical advantage around the ball zone.

The Double Marking is Unsuccessful But the Numerical Superiority Fixes the Problem

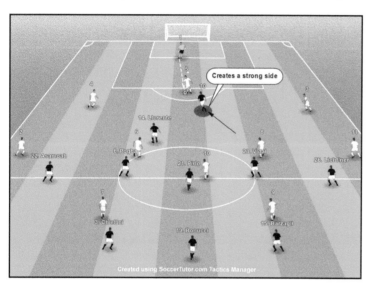

In this example the team's aim is to apply pressing.

As soon as the pass is made to white No.5 from the goalkeeper, Tevez (10) closes down the centre back in a way which blocks off the pass to No.3 and forces the ball towards the left side of Juventus (strong side created).

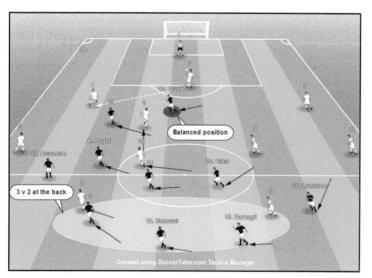

No.5 passes to No.4. All of the Juventus players shift towards the left.

Llorente (14) puts pressure on the new ball carrier. No.6 drops back so Tevez (10) takes up a balanced position to control both No.5 and No.6.

The white No.10 is in a deep position so Juventus have a 3 v 2 situation at the back.

The white No.4 passes out wide to No.2 - Asamoah (22) closes him down together with Pogba (6) who uses a well timed run to help double mark the new ball carrier.

The white No.10 drops deep to provide a potential passing option for No.2. Llorente (14) reads the tactical situation, moves into a balanced position, controls the potential pass towards No.10 and also blocks the pass to No.6.

Tevez moves close to the ball zone to create a numerical advantage (6 v 5) and provide help if necessary.

Despite the double marking and Llorente's positioning, No.2 still manages to pass inside to No.10.

As Juve had many players around the ball zone the available space for the whites was reduced.

When the No.10 receives he is immediately put under pressure by the three nearest players to him - Llorente (14), Tevez (10) and Pirlo (21).

Defending the Switch of Play When the Receiver Had Time On the Ball

In a similar situation to the previous one, the No.10 manages to receive and switch the play this time.

The next two diagrams show how Juventus responded to this tactical situation.

Lichtsteiner (the closest player to the new man in possession - No.11) has to evaluate the situation and decide if he should move to close him down.

There is a 4 v 2 situation at the back in favour of Juve which will become 3 v 2 if Lichtsteiner moves forward. However if this takes place immediately, No.9 will be free of marking for a couple of seconds as Barzagli (15) isn't far enough across. Additionally the opposition look to take advantage of the open ball situation and move to receive in behind. This means that all the defenders have to drop back to prevent this from happening.

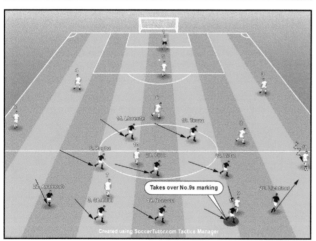

As Barzagli (15) has now taken over No.9's marking, Lichtsteiner (26) moves forward to put pressure on the ball. His aim should be to reduce the available time and space and force No.11 towards the sideline until Vidal (23) reaches an effective supporting position.

The wing back on the weak side (Asamoah) has also moved back while the midfielders and forwards have formed the correct shape and the team is well organised.

As soon as Lichtsteiner (26) manages to create a closed ball situation, the defenders should stop their backwards movement.

The Wing Back Drops Back When There is a 3 v 3 Situation at the Back

This situation is similar to the previous one but this time the white No.10 takes up a position behind Juve's midfield line.

As the No.10 is away from the strong side and not a potential receiver, the player who has to compensate for the potential 3 v 3 is the wing back on the weak side (No.26 - Lichtsteiner) who moves to be in line with him.

The right centre back (4) plays a long pass towards No.7. As Lichtsteiner has moved into an effective defensive position, Chiellini (3) is coached to contest the No.7 aggressively and try to reach the ball first.

Pogba (6) and Pirlo (21) move close to provide help and apply triple marking. Asamoah (22) and Bonucci (19) provide cover behind Chiellini and Juventus will most likely win the ball.

Coaching the Juventus 3-5-2: Defending

CHAPTER 7
DEFENDING AGAINST THE 3-5-2

DEFENDING AGAINST THE 3-5-2

In the diagrams to follow we show how Juventus defended against teams which used the 3-5-2 formation.

Defending in a Passive Way

When defending in a passive way, the Juventus players waited within the middle third for the opposition. At the same time they tried to retain a compact formation and block the potential through passes. If there was a successful through pass, the new player in possession would have little space to take advantage of, and he was immediately put under pressure.

Starting Positions

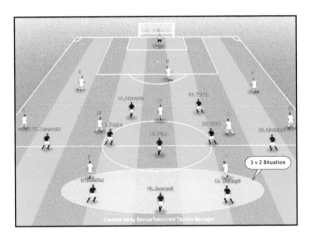

This diagram shows the positions of the players when the ball was in the opposition goalkeeper's possession.

Juventus retain a numerical advantage at the back with a 3 v 2 situation.

Starting Positions When the Ball is in the Left Centre Back's Possession

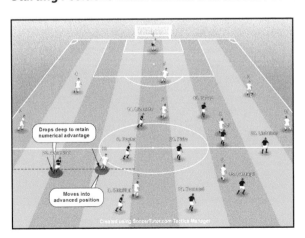

In this example the opposition's No.10 has moved into an advanced position ready to create a 3 v 3 situation at the back for Juventus.

The weak side's wing back Asamoah (22) reads the tactical situation and moves across and back to be in line with the white No.10, creating a numerical advantage at the back (4 v 3).

Coaching the Juventus 3-5-2: Defending

Double or Triple Marking of a Player Who Receives the Ball in the Centre of the Pitch

The pass is played from the goalkeeper to No.5 in the centre. The aim for Juventus is to defend in a passive way within the middle third.

The white centre back (5) moves forward and the Juventus players get more compact, narrow the potential passing lanes and get ready to block any through passes.

The white No.8 drops back to provide a passing option.

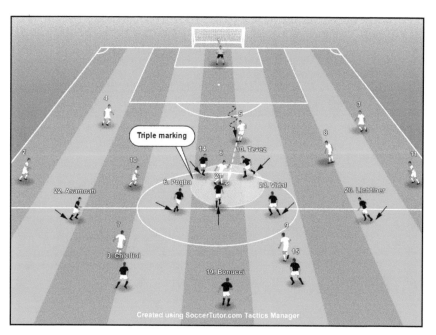

The white centre back (5) manages to make a successful pass to the centre midfielder (6) but the compact formation results in him being put under immediate pressure by 3 Juventus players - Llorente (14), Tevez (10) and Pirlo (21).

Defending in a Passive Way in the Centre: Getting Behind the Ball and Retaining a Good Shape With a Compact Formation

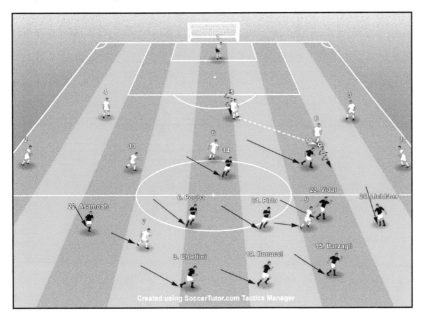

This diagram shows the reaction of the players if No.5 had chosen to pass to No.8 instead of No.6.

No.8 receives and attacks the space by moving forward with the ball. Vidal (23) doesn't move forward to put pressure on him but leaves Tevez (10) to take over his marking. Tevez tracks his run with the aim of closing him down and getting behind the ball again.

The rest of the players also drop back to keep a compact formation, retain a safety distance from the man in possession and get ready to block the potential through passes.

Tevez (10) manages to close No.8 down successfully and forces him to pass the ball out wide to No.11.

The Juve players stop their backward movement and take advantage of the transmission phase (the time it takes for the pass to travel from No.8 to No.11) to move a couple of yards forward, while still retaining a compact formation.

Coaching the Juventus 3-5-2: Defending

Pressing Against the 3-5-2

When pressing Juventus aimed to force the ball towards one side in order to create a strong side and then put pressure on the ball. At the same time they would make sure to mark all potential receivers and (if possible) create a numerical advantage around the ball zone.

All the Potential Receivers are Tightly Marked During the Pressing Application On the Right

Juventus' aim is to apply pressing high up the pitch. Llorente (14) presses in such a way as to block off the pass to No.4 and forces the ball one way which creates a strong side.

The ball is passed out wide to the left centre back (3). Tevez (10) puts pressure on him in a way that prevents the back pass to No.5. This enables Llorente (14) to drop back and shift towards the strong side close to No.6.

Vidal (23) and Barzagli (15) mark the potential receivers No.8 and No.9 tightly while Lichtsteiner (26) gets ready to put pressure on No.11.

The rest of the Juventus players shift towards the right.

The pass is directed out wide to No.11 and Lichtsteiner (26) puts him under pressure immediately.

Tevez (10) moves back to try and help double mark No.11 and all the potential receivers are marked tightly.

There is a 3 v 2 situation at the back and Juventus are well organised and balanced.

Defending the Switch of Play When the Receiver Has Time On the Ball

After 3 consecutive passes the white team successfully switch the play to Juve's weak side.

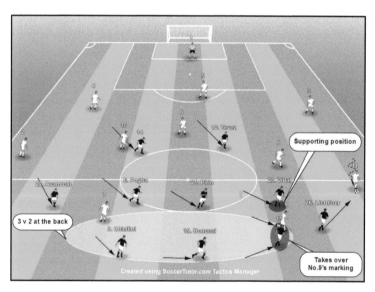

Juventus take advantage of the transmission phase (the time the ball takes to travel) and shift towards the right. No.11 receives and moves forward with the ball. There is an open ball situation but as the white forwards didn't move to receive a pass in behind the defensive line, the Juventus defenders don't have to move back.

Lichtsteiner (26) and the other Juventus defenders have to evaluate the tactical situation.

1. There is a 4 v 2 situation at the back which will become 3 v 2 if Lichtsteiner (26) moves forwards.

2. Vidal (23) is in position to provide support.

3. Barzagli (15) has taken advantage of the transmission phase and he is already close to No.9. This means that Lichtsteiner (26) can move forward and close the man in possession down.

Compensating for a 3 v 3 Situation at the Back

One way to cause problems for Juventus when playing with the 3-5-2 system was to move one of the midfielders into an advanced position to create a 3 v 3 situation in the highlighted area shown below in the diagram.

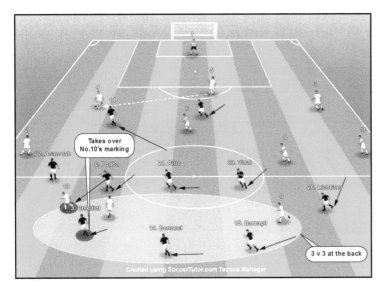

The ball is in the right centre back's (4) possession.

The white No.10 makes a run into the space behind Asamoah (22). Pogba (6) follows his run for a few yards while Chiellini (3) reads the tactical situation and gets ready to mark No.10. This would however leave the white No.7 free of marking.

Lichtsteiner (26) also reads the tactical situation and drops back to prevent an equality of numbers being created at the back (3 v 3). All of the other Juventus players shift towards the left.

Normally long passes are not very accurate and the defenders have enough time to prepare themselves to defend them comfortably. However, in this example No.4 plays an accurate long pass to No.10 who receives.

Communication is very important in these types of tactical situations. Chiellini (3) is coached to contest him with the aim of playing for time. As soon as either Asamoah (22) or Lichtsteiner (26) drops back into an effective defensive position, Chiellini can then contest No.10 more aggressively.

If Asamoah (22) was higher up the pitch and unable to drop back into a defensive position on time, Lichtsteiner's effective position would still be enough to trigger more aggressive defending from Chiellini. Pogba moves to help double mark No.10.

Coaching the Juventus 3-5-2: Defending

CHAPTER 8
DEFENDING AGAINST THE 4-2-3-1

DEFENDING AGAINST THE 4-2-3-1

In the diagrams to follow there are several situations analysed which show how Juventus defended against the 4-2-3-1 formation. When Juventus faced a team which used the 4-2-3-1 there were several adjustments to be made in order for the team to retain a numerical advantage at the back and not be too defensive at the same time.

The two wing backs could easily drop back and take over the marking of the opposition wingers, however this would be too defensive. It could be used when the team was winning and they were looking for retain their lead but in situations when the team had to attack this was not the best option.

The more defensively capable wing back Lichtsteiner (26) would drop into a deeper position and the left wing back (Asamoah - 22) would usually be in a more advanced position. This created a 4 v 3 situation at the back instead of a much more defensive 5 v 3 situation. There were of course times when the right wing back Lichtsteiner moved forward and put pressure on the opposition's full back and Asamoah dropped deeper but this was not very frequent.

A problem for Juventus could occur if the opposition's attacking midfielder moved into an advanced position. This would then create a 4 v 4 situation at the back and Juventus had to make some adjustments to compensate for this.

Defending in a Passive Way

When defending in a passive way, the Juventus players waited within the middle third for the opposition. At the same time they tried to retain a compact formation and block the potential through passes. If there was a successful through pass, the new player in possession would have little time or space to take advantage of, and he was immediately put under pressure.

Starting Positions With the Ball in the Goalkeeper's Possession

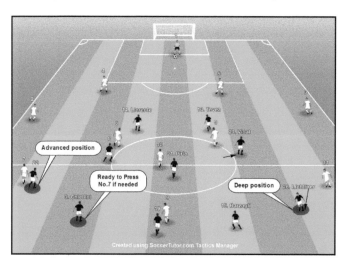

In this diagram we show the starting positions of the Juventus players against a team that uses the 4-2-3-1 formation.

There is a 5 v 3 situation at the back which provides safety. However the left wing back Asamoah (22) is higher up the pitch and Lichtsteiner (26) drops into a deeper position.

This meant that there were many times that Asamoah moved forward to put pressure on the opposing right back (when he had the ball) and Chiellini (3) would take over No.7's marking, with Juve switching to a 4 v 3 situation at the back.

Starting Positions With the Ball in the Right Centre Back's Possession

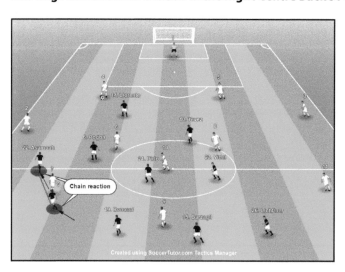

The left wing back Asamoah (22) takes up a more advanced position here so if the pass is directed to the right back (2) he will be the first player to put pressure on the ball.

The white No.7's position is towards the centre and he is left under Chiellini's (3) marking (in a chain reaction) as the distances between the players are short. This chain reaction was the usual response of the players when the opposition attacked on Juve's left side.

Although this was the most common reaction, there were also times when Pogba (6) was the first player to put pressure on the opposition right back when Asamoah was in a deeper position.

Starting Positions With the Ball in the Left Centre Back's Possession

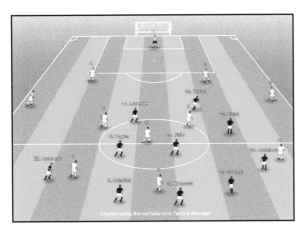

When the ball was in the left centre back's possession the starting positions were as shown in the diagram.

Vidal (23) takes up a wider position to be close to the opposition's left back and Lichtsteiner (26) remains in a deep position marking No.11.

Asamoah (22) doesn't have to drop deeper unless the situation at the back changes.

Starting Positions Against 3 Narrow Forwards

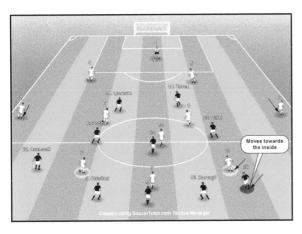

If the two opposition wingers (7 and 11) were in narrow positions, the right wing back Lichtsteiner (26) moved towards the centre to compensate and help provide balance at the back.

Starting Positions When the Attacking Midfielder is in an Advanced Position

The ball is in the goalkeeper's possession again.

The white No.10 moves into a more advanced position behind the Juventus midfield line and creates a 4 v 4 situation at the back for Juventus.

The left wing back Asamoah (22) reads the tactical situation and drops back to help retain a numerical advantage (5 v 4).

Defending in a Passive Way Within the Middle Third (Variation 1): Blocking the Through Ball

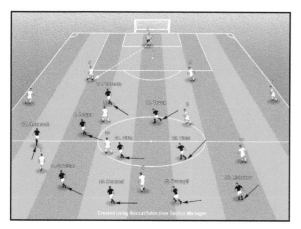

In this example Juventus are defending passively in the middle third.

The players all shift towards the left and retain a compact formation.

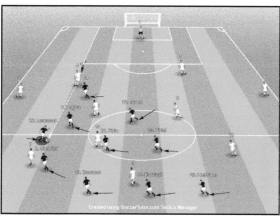

As the player with the ball (4) moves forward the Juventus players gather around the ball zone and create a more compact formation. This results in even shorter distances between the players and narrower passing lanes for the opposition.

The white centre back (4) passes towards No.7 and Asamoah (22) intercepts the ball.

Defending in a Passive Way Within the Middle Third (Variation 2): Triple Marking Against a Player Who Receives a Horizontal Pass in the Centre

In this variation to the previous example, the centre back (4) chooses to pass out wide to the right back (2) this time. All of the Juventus players shift towards the left.

The passing lanes become narrower and the spaces become limited for the opposition.

Coaching the Juventus 3-5-2: Defending

The right back (2) manages to make a pass through a narrow passing lane inside to No.6. However there is a lack of any space and the No.6 is immediately blocked by 3 Juventus players - Llorente (14), Pogba (6) and Tevez (10).

Additionally Pirlo (21) marks No.10 tightly to prevent him becoming a passing option and Vidal (23) gets closer to the ball zone. Both of them are ready to intervene if necessary.

Defending in a Passive Way Within the Middle Third (Variation 3): Triple Marking Against a Player Who Receives a Diagonal Pass in the Centre

In this third variation the right back (2) is able to make a successful pass to the No.10.

The new man in possession (10) is immediately put under pressure by 3 Juventus players - Pogba (6), Tevez (10) and Pirlo (21).

Pirlo contests No.10 aggressively with the aim of forcing him into a bad first touch.

Pressing Against the 4-2-3-1

When pressing, Juventus aimed to force the ball towards one side in order to create a strong side and then put pressure on the ball. At the same time they would mark all potential receivers and (if possible) create a numerical advantage around the ball zone.

Pressing On the Left and Creating a Numerical Advantage Around the Ball Zone

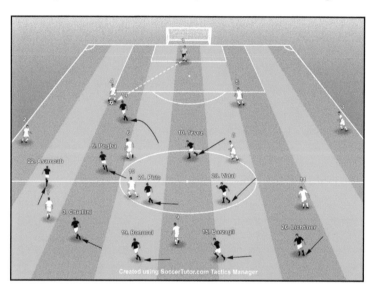

Llorente (14) puts pressure on the ball with a curved run to create a strong side. As one side of the pitch is blocked off, Tevez is able to drop back and towards the strong side to keep the team compact.

The rest of the Juventus players shift towards the left. Pogba (6) and Asamoah (22) are ready to block a potential through pass.

The pass is played to the right back (2). Juventus have achieved all their aims when pressing so Asamoah (22) and Pogba (6) move to double mark the new man in possession. Llorente (14) moves into a balanced position to control both the back pass and the potential pass to No.6.

Chiellini (3) and Pirlo (21) mark the potential receivers No.7 and No.10 tightly and there is superiority in numbers around the ball. Furthermore all of the Juve defenders are able to aggressively mark their direct opponents if the ball is directed towards them. This is because the tactical situation (4 v 3) favours it.

If the right back (2) manages to find a way to pass the ball to No.7, the numerical superiority for Juventus around the ball zone prevents the opposition from progressing.

Specifically Chiellini (3) moves forwards to contest No.7 aggressively, and Asamoah (22) and Pirlo (21) move to help triple mark the winger.

Preventing a Numerical Equality Occurring at the Back When Pressing On the Left

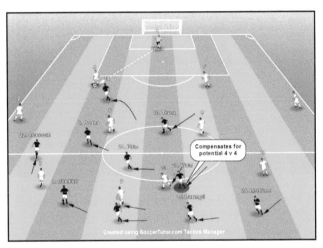

Llorente (14) puts pressure on the ball with a curved run to create a strong side again.

Asamoah is already in an advanced position and there is a 4 v 3 situation at the back for Juventus.

The opposition's No.10 moves into an advanced position behind Pirlo (21) so Vidal (23) follows his movement and gets closer to the defenders. This movement by Vidal prevents a 4 v 4 situation from occurring at the back for Juventus.

The right centre back (4) plays a long pass to the forward (9). If the pass is accurate and Bonucci (19) is unable to reach the ball first, he should hold up No.9 and play for time, making sure that the forward is unable to turn.

Vidal (23) who is already close to the defenders moves across to help Bonucci and double mark the forward (9).

With this response either possession will be won or time will be gained, enabling the left wing back Asamoah (22) to recover into an effective position and thus creating a 5 v 4 numerical advantage at the back.

Defending the Switch Of Play When the Receiver Has Time On the Ball

In this situation the opposition are able to switch the play towards the other side. The left back receives the ball in space.

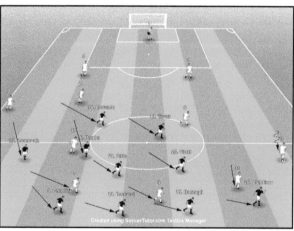

The Juventus players all shift towards the right and No.3 moves forwards with the ball. There is an open ball situation and the opposition forwards move forward to receive. The Juve defenders have to prevent passes in behind by dropping back and shifting to the right.

The right wing back Lichtsteiner (26) does not move forward to put pressure on the ball as the 4 v 3 situation would become 3 v 3 (Asamoah is in an advanced position). Lichtsteiner also gives time to the midfielders to shift closer to the defenders and create a compact formation to compensate for the 3 v 3. Time is also given for Barzagli (15) to shift across and take over No.11's marking.

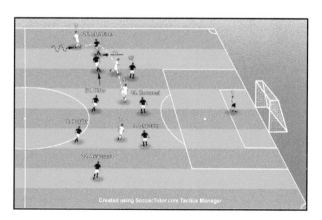

Barzagli (15) has moved close to Lichtsteiner (26) and the switch in No.11's marking has been achieved. The Juve midfielders are close to the defenders and ready to provide help. Vidal (23) has moved into a supporting position and Asamoah is on his way to take up a more effective position and provide help at the back.

As a result Lichtsteiner (26) is now coached to move forward and put pressure on the player in possession (3). As the Juventus players have neutralised the possibility of a pass in behind, the opposition left back (3) is forced to play an aerial pass inside to the forward (9).

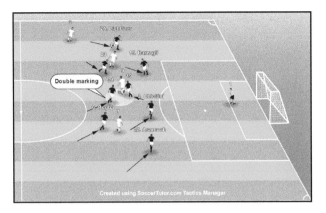

As soon as the ball is directed to No.9, Bonucci (19) moves forward to contest him (not aggressively) with the aim of preventing him from turning.

Pirlo (21) moves back and provides help. Either possession will be won or time will be given for Asamoah (22) to recover into an effective defensive position. As soon as this occurs, Bonucci (19) can then switch to more aggressive defending.

The Attacking Midfielder Moves Into an Advanced Position When Pressing On the Left
(5 v 3 Situation at the Back)

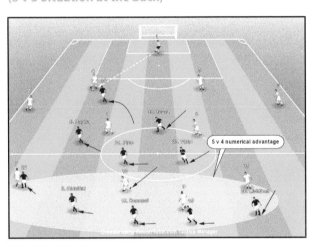

In this situation the centre back (4) receives a pass from the goalkeeper. The Juventus players all shift towards the left.

This time Asamoah (22) is in a deep position with a player to mark (No.7). This is a defensive minded formation (5 v 3 at back) but it can happen even if the coach's plan is different. The white No.10 moves forwards behind Pirlo (21). Vidal (23) reads the tactical situation (deep position of Asamoah) and leaves him under the defenders' supervision without following him. The situation becomes 5 v 4 but there is still a numerical advantage for Juventus at the back.

As soon as the pass is played to the right back (2), Pogba (6) puts pressure on him.

White No.6 drops back to provide a passing option. Despite Pirlo's (21) movement forwards (chain reaction) he is still too far away from No.6, so Llorente (14) moves back to block the potential pass towards him.

The Juventus defenders all shift towards the left and Asamoah (22) marks No.7 very tightly as he is a potential receiver.

Coaching the Juventus 3-5-2: Defending

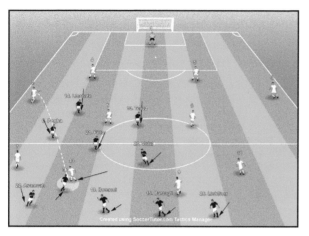

As the pass to No.6 is covered, the right back (2) plays a long pass towards No.10. Chiellini (3) moves to aggressively contest him as the situation favours it (numerical advantage at the back).

The left wing back Asamoah (22) and Bonucci (19) provide cover immediately and the defensive line is well organised and balanced.

All Potential Receivers are Tightly Marked in a Balanced Situation When Pressing On the Right

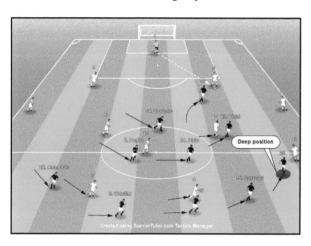

In this situation Juventus are pressing on the right. Tevez (10) puts pressure on the ball and creates a strong side by using a curved run.

As we have already mentioned, the right wing back Lichtsteiner (26) was most often in a more defensive position than the left wing back Asamoah (22). This positioning forces Vidal (23) to get ready to put pressure on the ball if the pass is directed to the left back (3).

This starts a chain reaction as Lichtsteiner has to move forwards to mark No.11. The other Juve defenders shift across and Asamoah drops back.

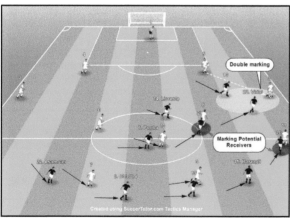

As soon as the centre back (5) passes to the left back (3), Vidal (23) moves to close him down and Pirlo (21) moves forwards to mark No.8 (chain reaction). As Lichtsteiner is also marking No.11 all potential receivers are tightly marked.

Tevez (10) drops back to help double mark the ball carrier and blocks the pass back to No.5.

There is a 4 v 3 numerical advantage at the back and Asamoah (22) is in a position to drop further back if required. This is a balanced situation for Juventus and there is no need for any adjustments to be made.

Defending the Switch of Play When the Receiver Has Time On the Ball

After three consecutive passes the white team successfully switch the play towards the right back (2).

The right back (2) receives and moves forward. There is an open ball situation so the defenders shift towards the left and also move backwards. The forwards want to receive in behind. There is a 5 v 3 situation at the back and if Asamoah (22) moves forward it becomes 4 v 3.

Chiellini (3) has taken advantage of the transmission phase and taken over No.7's marking. Pogba (6) has moved closer and gets ready to support Asamoah. All these factors favour applying immediate pressure on the player in possession, so Asamoah moves forward to reduce his available time and space.

Takes over No7's marking

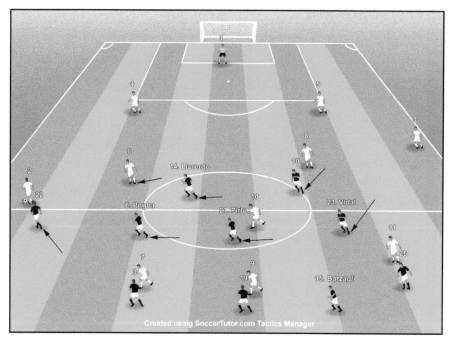

Asamoah (22) closes No.2 down and forces him to shield the ball.

As there is now a closed ball situation, the Juventus defenders stop their backward movement and the midfielders continue to shift across to the left.

When No.2 passes back to No.6, the Juventus defenders take advantage of the transmission phase (the time the ball takes to travel) and quickly step up a couple of yards, leaving the opposition forwards in offside positions.

The team is now compact, with good shape and balance.

CHAPTER 9
DEFENDING AGAINST THE 4-4-2

DEFENDING AGAINST THE 4-4-2

When defending against a team using the 4-4-2 formation, Juventus had a numerical advantage at the back (3 v 2). The player who moved forward to put pressure on the full back in possession was usually the attacking midfielder (Marchisio or Vidal). However there were times when the wing back on the strong side took over this role, but this was a reaction that could only take place under certain circumstances.

Juventus had to make some adjustments when an opposing midfield player moved forwards and created a 3 v 3 situation at the back. These situations are going to be analysed in the following diagrams.

Defending in a Passive Way

When defending in a passive way, Juventus players waited within the middle third for the opposition. At the same time they tried to retain a compact formation and block the potential through passes. If there was a successful through pass, the new player in possession had little space to take advantage of, and he was immediately put under pressure.

Starting Positions (The Ball is in the Goalkeeper's Possession)

The starting positions of the Juventus players against the 4-4-2 formation are shown in the diagram. The team is balanced and there are no adjustments needed to deal with the 4-4-2 formation.

Defending in a Passive Way Within the Middle Third: Double Marking the Winger Near the Sideline

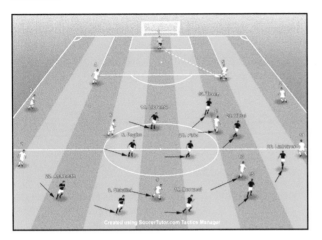

In this example the goalkeeper passes to the centre back (5). All of the Juventus players shift towards the right with the aim of defending passively by waiting for the opposition to enter the middle third.

The players retain a compact formation and block the potential through passes. The players get ready to defend against the pass towards the left back (3) as this is the most likely option.

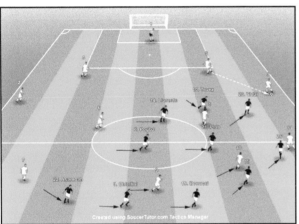

The pass is directed to the left back (3). Vidal (23) moves towards the new ball carrier but not too close as his focus is to retain a compact formation.

Tevez (10) drops back a couple of yards to control No.8 and prevent a pass being played inside.

Pirlo (21) and Pogba (6) shift across as part of a chain reaction while Lichtsteiner (26) marks No.11 closely.

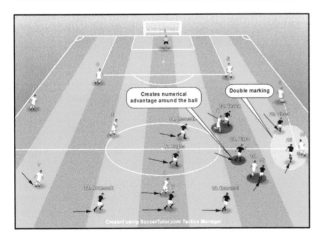

Juventus are able to retain a compact formation with short distances between the players. The white left back (3) passes the ball up the line to No.11 and Lichtsteiner (26) puts him under pressure immediately, preventing him from turning.

Vidal (23) drops back to help Lichtsteiner double mark No.11 while Barzagli (15) marks No.10 tightly and Tevez (10) is ready to block a pass towards No.8.

Pirlo (21) moves close to the ball zone and helps to create a numerical superiority in that area. With the players' positioning it is very likely that Juventus will win possession.

Pressing Against the 4-4-2

When pressing, the aim for Juventus was to force the ball towards one side in order to create a strong side and then put pressure on the ball. At the same time they mark all potential receivers and (if possible) create a numerical advantage around the ball zone.

Marking All the Potential Receivers (and Double Marking) When Pressing On the Left

As soon as the ball is passed from the goalkeeper, Llorente (14) moves to apply pressure on the centre back (4) and creates a strong side, forcing the play to Juventus' left side.

The next pass is played to the right back (2). Pogba (6) puts pressure on him and Pirlo (21) moves forwards to mark No.6 as part of a chain reaction.

Llorente (14) drops back to double mark the right back (2) and Asamoah (22) marks No.7 tightly. Tevez is ready to provide help if the pass is directed to No.6.

All the potential receivers of the ball are closely marked and there is also double marking of the player in possession. This was the ideal situation for Juventus in the defensive phase.

Coaching the Juventus 3-5-2: Defending

Defending With a 5 v 5 Situation at the Back When Pressing On the Left

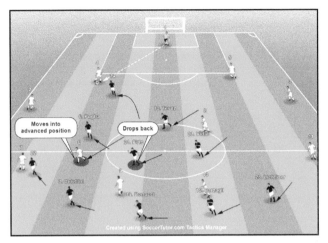

This situation presented was one that could trouble Juventus. One of the centre midfielders (No.6 in the diagram) moves forward behind Pogba's back. This creates a 5 v 5 situation at the back for Juve.

Pirlo (21) is aware of the danger and follows his movement for a couple of yards. However this is not to mark him but just to get closer to the defenders.

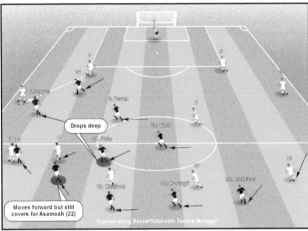

The pass is directed to the right back (2). Pogba (6) moves forward to put pressure on him and Llorente (14) moves back.

The left wing back Asamoah (22) moves forward to mark No.7 and Chiellini (3) moves close to No.6 - this forward movement by Chiellini allows him to mark No.6 and be in a covering position for Asamoah.

Pirlo (21) sees that Chiellini is out of position so he moves even closer to the defenders and No.6.

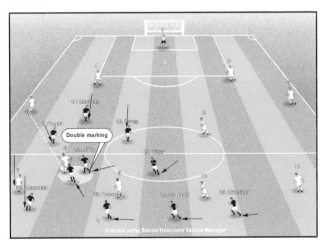

The right back (2) passes to the centre midfielder (6) and he is immediately put under pressure by Chiellini (3) with Pirlo (21) also moving across to help apply double marking .

These defensive movements from Chiellini and Pirlo compensate for the 5 v 5 equality in numbers at the back. Asamoah (22) and Bonucci (19) provide cover.

This situation should lead to Juventus winning possession. If it was not orchestrated correctly, the man in possession could turn to face Juventus' goal with an equality in numbers and a good chance for the opposition to score.

Defending the Switch of Play When the Receiver Has Time On the Ball

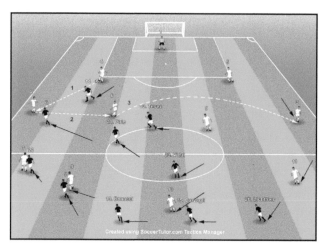

The white team manages to switch play successfully.

The Juventus players at the back retain short distances between each other and this makes the shifting of the opponent's marking much easier.

In addition, as Asamoah (22) is not in an advanced position, dropping into an effective defensive position will not take long.

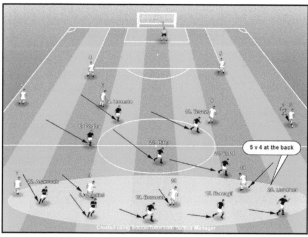

No.3 receives and moves forward with plenty of space in front of him. As there is an open ball situation and the forwards move to receive a pass in behind, the Juventus defenders move backwards to prevent this. Barzagli (15) has to shift a few yards to take over No.11's marking.

There is a 5 v 4 situation at the back that could become 4 v 4 if Lichtsteiner (26) moves forward. As the man in possession is still quite deep, Vidal (23) has time to shift across and take over the role of the first defender.

A numerical advantage is retained at the back and Barzagli (15) has time to mark No.11.

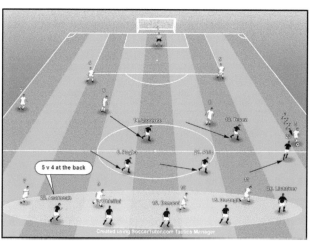

As soon as Vidal (23) closes the left back (3) down and the forward pass is no longer possible, the defenders stop their backward movement.

The team is now balanced with a 5 v 4 situation at the back. They retain a good shape.

If Vidal (23) was too far away to be the first defender, Lichtsteiner (26) would have moved forwards to put pressure on the ball as soon as the midfielders recovered into an effective position close to the defenders. This would form a compact formation to compensate for the equality in numbers at the back (4 v 4).

CHAPTER 10
DEFENDING AGAINST THE 4-3-3

DEFENDING AGAINST THE 4-3-3

Against the 4-3-3 formation Juventus needed to make sure that they did not to form a defensive minded formation with 5 v 3 at the back, so one of the two wing backs (usually Asamoah - the left wing back) stayed in an advanced position while the other one (usually Lichtsteiner- the right wing back) dropped into a more defensive position. Juventus formed a four men defence with Asamoah moving forward to put pressure on the opposition's right back when he had the ball.

Defending in a Passive Way

When defending in a passive way, the Juventus players waited within the middle third for the opposition. At the same time they tried to retain a compact formation and block the potential through passes. If there was a successful through pass, the new player in possession had little time or space to take advantage of, and he was immediately put under pressure.

Starting Positions (The Ball is in the Goalkeeper's Possession)

The starting positions against the 4-3-3 formation are shown in this diagram.

The right wing back Lichtsteiner (26) dropped a few yards back in order to take up a more defensive position while the left wing back Asamoah (22) was in a more advanced position. Vidal moved slightly towards the right to be closer to the opposition's left back.

These adjustments were made in order to create a four man defence which is more attack minded than having five players at the back.

Defending in a Passive Way Within the Middle Third (Option 1): Triple Marking the Winger

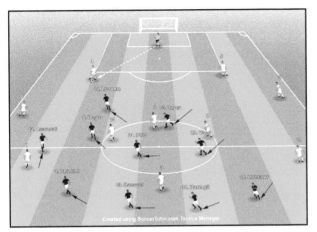

Juventus' aim is to defend passively in the middle third. The goalkeeper passes to No.4 and Llorente (14) moves close to him. The other players shift to the left. Pogba (6) and Asamoah (22) block the forward passing options while the other players gather around the ball zone and retain a compact formation.

Asamoah moves forwards and is ready to close No.2 down if the pass is directed to him and blocks the pass to No.7 at the same time. No.7 can only receive a long pass through a narrow passing lane. Asamoah and Pogba retain a safe distance from the ball carrier.

The pass is played to the right back (2) and Asamoah (22) moves to close him down as he is closer to him than Pogba (6).

The other players shift towards the left and create superiority in numbers around the ball zone, while also blocking the potential receivers within the middle third. This is why Llorente (14) drops back instead of blocking the back pass.

The passing lanes towards the potential receivers are getting narrower and only the back pass (not dangerous) is left free.

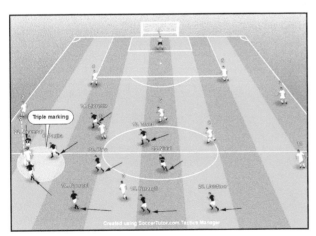

The right back (2) passes down the line to No.7. Chiellini (3) immediately puts him under pressure and prevents him from turning.

Asamoah (22) moves back and because the Juventus defenders have maintained short distances between each other he can help to double mark No.7 within just a few seconds.

Pogba also moves across to triple mark the ball carrier. It is again very likely that Juventus will win possession.

©SoccerTutor.com

Coaching the Juventus 3-5-2: Defending

Defending in a Passive Way Within the Middle Third (Option 2): Blocking the Horizontal Pass

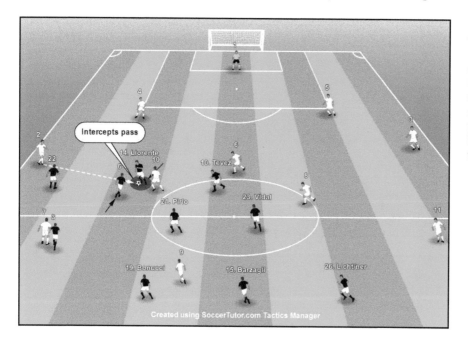

In this diagram the pass from the right back (2) is directed to No.10 but both Pogba (6) and Llorente (14) move to block the pass and Llorente is able to intercept the ball.

Defending in a Passive Way Within the Middle Third (Option 3): Blocking the Diagonal Pass

Finally in this example the right back (2) tries a diagonal pass towards the forward (9). The passing lane is narrow and both Pogba (6) and Pirlo (21) try to block it.

Pirlo has more time available to react and he is the one who succeeds in intercepting the ball.

Coaching the Juventus 3-5-2: Defending

Pressing Against the 4-3-3

When pressing the aim for Juventus was to force the ball towards one side in order to create a strong side and then put pressure on the ball. At the same time they mark all potential receivers and (if possible) create a numerical advantage around the ball zone.

The Wing Back Puts Pressure On the Full Back in an Advanced Position When Pressing On the Left

As soon as the ball is passed to No.4, Llorente (14) applies pressure and creates a strong side to force the play towards the left. The other Juve players shift towards the strong side created.

Pogba (6) moves to block the through pass and control No.6 who makes a movement to receive. Pirlo (6) follows No.10 (who makes a run behind Pogba) for a few yards to compensate for a potential 4 v 4 situation being created at the back - Asamoah is in an advanced position. Asamoah (22) gets ready to put pressure on the right back (2) in case he receives the ball.

The pass is played to the right back (2) and Asamoah puts pressure on him. Llorente (14) drops back to help double mark him.

Pogba (6) decides that it is not the right time for him to also close down the ball carrier so stays in a supporting position next to No.6 who moves to receive a pass.

Pirlo (21) and Chiellini (3) mark the other potential receivers of the ball (No.10 and No.7) tightly, while the other defenders retain superiority in numbers at the back.

Passing On the Marking of Forwards That Drop Deep to Receive

In this example No.8 moves into an advanced position on the weak side. This movement is going to create a 4 v 4 situation at the back for Juve so Vidal (23) is told to drop a few yards back.

The opposition's right winger (7) moves towards the centre into the potential passing lane. Chiellini (3) stays close to him but also stays close to the other defenders to maintain the numerical advantage at the back.

As the white No.8 moves into a more advanced position, Vidal (23) drops even closer to the defenders. Bonucci (19) tells Chiellini (3) not to track No.7 and Pogba (6) takes over his marking.

As soon as the pass is directed to the right back (2), Juve's left wing back Asamoah (22) moves to close him down. Llorente (14) takes up a balanced position between No.4 and No.10.

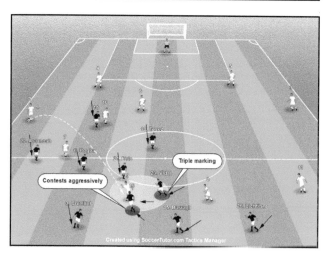

The right back (2) plays a long pass towards the forward No.9 and Bonucci (19) contests him to try and win the ball as the situation favours it.

Vidal (23) moves to help double mark the No.9 and Pirlo drops back to potentially help apply triple marking.

The other players at the back provide cover and balance. It is very likely that Juventus will win possession in this situation.

Aggressive Marking of the Forward When Pressing On the Right

In this diagram the pressing takes place on Juve's right side after the goalkeeper's pass to the centre back (5).

Tevez (10) moves to put pressure on the ball and create a strong side. The other players all shift towards the right.

Vidal (23) is in a position that enables him to block a potential through pass as well as put pressure on the left back (3) if the ball is directed to him.

As there is a 4 v 3 numerical advantage at the back, Asamoah (22) does not drop very deep.

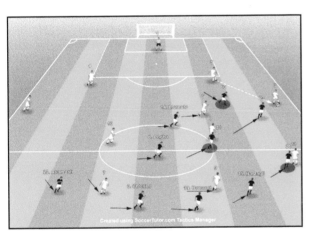

No.5 passes to the left back (3) and Vidal (23) moves to close him down. No.21 Pirlo (as part of a chain reaction) moves across to mark No.8.

Tevez (10) reads the tactical situation and takes up a balanced position to control both the pass back to the centre back (5) and the pass to No.6 who is also a potential receiver.

Juve's right wing back Lichtsteiner (26) moves forward and marks No.11 tightly. The other defenders all shift towards the strong side.

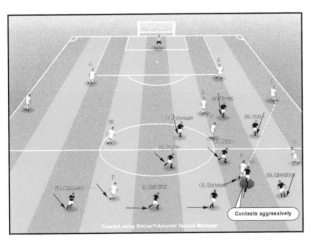

Contests aggressively

The left back (3) succeeds in passing the ball to the forward (9). Barzagli (15) immediately moves to contest him aggressively as the situation favours it.

Pirlo (21) is in an advanced position, so he drops back to provide help. Lichtsteiner (26) and Bonucci (19) both move inwards from their respective positions to provide cover behind Barzagli (15).

Asamoah (22) also moves back into the defensive line to provide more safety. Juventus are well balanced and organised.

Creating Superiority in Numbers On the Right Side

In this example the No.8 moves into an advanced position. The pass is played to No.3 and Vidal (23) puts pressure on him. Tevez (10) drops to help double mark.

As the strong side's wing back (Lichtsteiner - 26) is in a deep position, Pirlo (21) moves close to white No.6 and leaves No.8 under Barzagli's (15) supervision. Barzagli steps up to control No.8 but also stays in a covering position for Lichtsteiner.

Asamoah (22) has to drop back and help to retain the 5 v 4 numerical advantage at the back. This enables the defenders to contest their direct opponents aggressively.

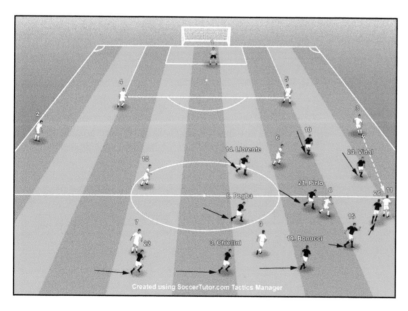

The left back (3) passes down the line to the winger (11). Juve's right wing back Lichtsteiner (26) contests No.11 aggressively and without hesitation, preventing him from being able to turn.

Vidal (23) moves back to try and help double mark No.11. Barzagli (15) is focused on providing cover behind Lichtsteiner and Pirlo (21) takes over No.8's marking.

Asamoah is already in an effective position and there is a 5 v 4 situation at the back. Juventus have a numerical advantage at the back and around the ball zone - it is very likely that they will win possession.

CHAPTER 11
DEFENDING AGAINST THE 4-3-1-2

DEFENDING AGAINST THE 4-3-1-2

Against the 4-3-1-2 formation, Juventus would retain a spare man at the back with a 3 v 2 advantage. When the opposition had the ball in the centre of the pitch and their No.10 moved into a more advanced position (creating a 3 v 3), the right wing back Lichtsteiner (26) dropped into a more defensive position. If the player with the ball was near the sideline, the player who dropped back to create a 4 v 3 was always the wing back on the weak side.

Defending in a Passive Way

When defending in a passive way, the Juventus players waited within the middle third for the opposition. At the same time they tried to retain a compact formation and block the potential through passes. If there was a successful through pass, the new player in possession had little time or space to take advantage of, and he was immediately put under pressure.

Starting Positions (The Ball is in the Goalkeeper's Possession)

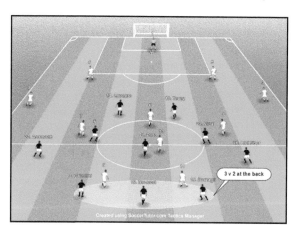

The ball is in the goalkeeper's possession and Juventus' positioning against the 4-3-1-2 is shown in the diagram.

Juventus have a 3 v 2 numerical advantage at the back.

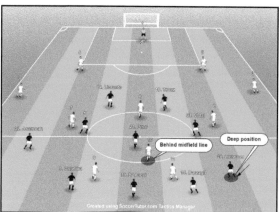

In this variation, the opposition No.10 takes up a more advanced position behind the Juventus midfield line.

Lichtsteiner (26) drops back into a more defensive position to create a four man defence. A numerical advantage at the back is maintained (4 v 3).

Coaching the Juventus 3-5-2: Defending

Defending in a Passive Way (Option 1): Double Marking in the Centre of the Pitch

In this situation Juventus aim to defend passively in the middle third. As soon as the ball is passed from the goalkeeper to the centre back (4,) the Juve players shift towards the left and retain a compact formation.

Pogba (6) and Asamoah (22) block the potential passing lane to the forward (No.9) and Tevez (10) moves across to block the passing lane to the white No.10 in the centre of the pitch.

The positioning of the Juve players forces the ball either towards the sideline, towards the other centre back (5) or to the defensive midfielder (6) who drops back to receive.

The centre back (4) decides to pass the ball to the defensive midfielder (6).

The Juventus players adjust their positioning to try and block potential through passes. If a through pass is successful they will be in good positions to be able to double mark the new man in possession.

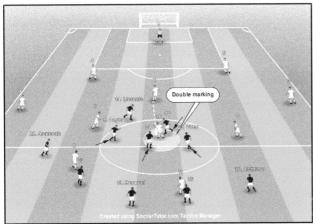
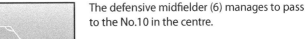

The defensive midfielder (6) manages to pass to the No.10 in the centre.

As the Juventus players have retained a compact formation with short distances between each other, the new ball carrier is immediately double marked by Tevez (10) and Pirlo (21).

In addition Vidal (23), Pogba (6) and Llorente (14) are all able to move close to the ball zone. There is no escape for the white No.10 and he loses possession.

Defending in a Passive Way (Option 2): Dropping Back Behind the Ball and Retaining a Compact Formation

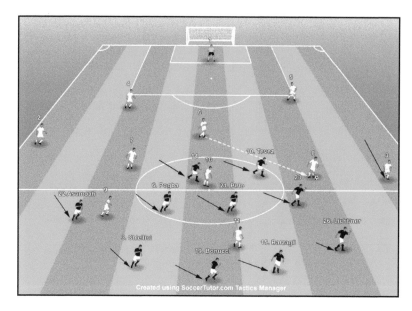

In this variation to the previous situation, the defensive midfielder (6) chooses to pass to No.8 instead of the No.10. This is a much more effective pass as No.8 can receive in space and has an easy passing option to the left back (3) on the flank.

All of the Juventus players read the tactical situation, drop back in synchronisation and readjust their positions. With this reaction Juventus are able to get 8 players behind the ball and the 2 forwards also help by tracking back to defend.

The team retain a good shape and a compact formation.

No.8 passes to the advanced left back (3). The Juventus defenders shift towards the right and retain short distances between each other.

Lichtsteiner (26) is the closest player to No.3 and moves to put pressure on the ball as there is already numerical advantage at the back (4 v 2) and the midfielders have taken up effective positions close to the defenders. Juventus have created a very compact block

The forwards also shift towards the right and Juve are well organised and balanced.

Retaining a Compact Formation When Defending Passively Near the Sideline (Option 1):
Double or Triple Marking of the Forward

In this example the centre back (4) passes the ball out wide to the right back (2). The Juventus players all shift towards the left and get ready to defend against any through passes.

If the opposition are able to complete a successful pass then the short distances between the players will enable the players to apply double or in some cases triple marking as soon as a player receives.

Despite the narrow passing lane, the right back (2) manages to pass to the forward (9).

No.9 is immediately put under pressure by Chiellini (3) and Pirlo (21). Pogba (6) and Asamoah (22) also move close to the ball zone.

The No.9 is completely surrounded and loses possession.

Retaining a Compact Formation When Defending Passively Near the Sideline (Option 2):
Anticipating Danger and Marking Players in Advance

In this variation to the previous example, the No.9 moves towards the sideline to receive the pass from the right back (2).

As Chiellini (3) is already marking No.9 in advance of his movement, he is in position to move quickly towards the ball and win possession.

Retaining a Compact Formation When Defending Passively Near the Sideline (Option 3):
Blocking an Inside Pass or Double Marking the New Ball Carrier

In this final variation of this situation, the right back (2) passes inside to No.7.

Pogba (6) moves forwards to try and block the pass. If he does not successfully intercept the ball, he still puts pressure on the new man in possession together with Llorente (14).

Pressing Against the 4-3-1-2

When pressing, Juventus aimed to force the ball towards one side in order to create a strong side and then put pressure on the ball. At the same time they would mark all potential receivers and (if possible) create a numerical advantage around the ball zone.

Aggressive Marking and Double Marking the Forward When Pressing On the Left

In this situation Juventus are pressing high up the pitch.

Llorente (14) is the first player to apply pressure on the ball. The white right back (2) is in a deep position.

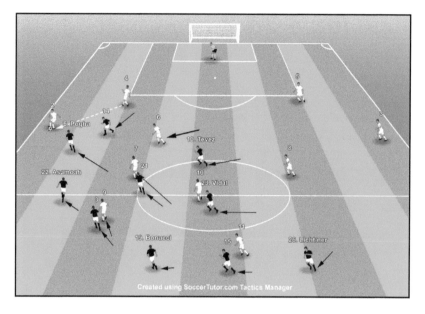

The centre back (4) passes to the right back (2). As Asamoah (22) is in a deep position, the first player to put pressure on him is Pogba (6).

Llorente (14) moves to help double mark him as well as block the potential pass to the defensive midfielder (6) who is in a deep position and moves to provide a passing option.

Pirlo (21) follows Pogba as part of a chain reaction and marks No.7. The left wing back Asamoah (22) stays close to the defenders and is in position to try and block the potential through pass. The right wing back Lichtsteiner (26) drops back to provide safety in numbers at the back.

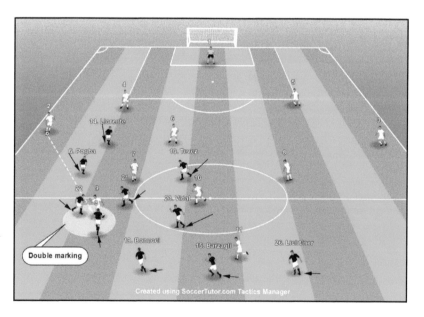

The right back (2) manages to pass through the narrow passing lane to the forward (9).

No.9 is aggressively contested by Chiellini (3). Asamoah (22) has no direct opponent to mark, so drops back to help double mark No.9.

Pirlo (21) also moves to provide help and it is very likely that Juventus will win possession.

Restoring Compactness

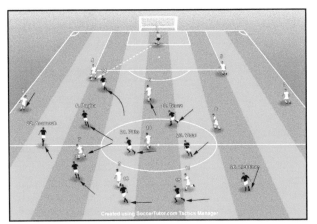

In this situation the right back (2) is in a more advanced position as the pass is directed to the centre back (4) from the goalkeeper. Juve's left wing back Asamoah (22) is closer to him in this situation.

All of the Juventus players shift towards the left and the white No.7 moves towards the sideline to create width.

This can create a 3 v 3 situation at the back but it is the wing back on the weak side (Lichtsteiner) who has the responsibility to drop back and restore a 4 v 3 numerical advantage.

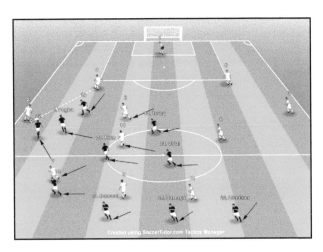

The pass is played to the right back (2) and Asamoah (22) moves to close him down. Pogba (6) moves to help double mark him and Llorente (14) drops back to block the potential pass to the defensive midfielder (6) who moves to receive.

No.7 continues his run towards the sideline and Chiellini (3) takes over his marking. Bonucci (19) moves back to provide cover for Chiellini and the rest of the defenders drop back to retain their shape. However, this response increases the distance between the defenders and midfielders and the team loses their compactness.

The right back (2) passes inside to the defensive midfielder (6). Tevez (10) puts him under pressure and Llorente (14) is near the ball zone to provide help.

Pirlo (21) moves close to No.10 (potential receiver) and the other midfielders move into positions just behind Pirlo (21) in order to form the correct team shape.

The most important element in this situation is that the defenders take advantage of the transmission phase (time the ball takes to travel) to move forward together and restore the compactness. The team is now well organised and Juventus have the correct shape to defend.

Coaching the Juventus 3-5-2: Defending

Defending When 2 Midfielders Move into Advanced Positions

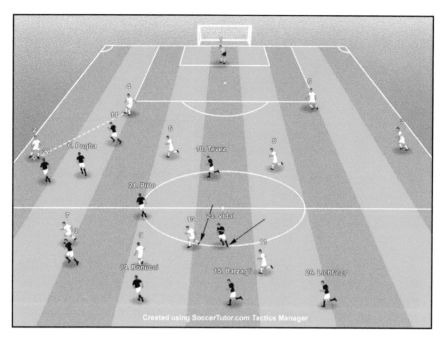

This diagram shows a variation of the previous situation.

This time the white No.10 also moves into an advanced as well as No.7.

Vidal (23) knows that this movement will create a 4 v 4 situation at the back so he drops back to be closer to the defence.

The pass is played from the right back (2) to No.7. Chiellini (3) is coached by his teammates and contests No.7 with the aim of playing for time. This gives the left wing back Asamoah (22) time to move into a supporting position as well as giving Vidal (23) time to drop further back.

As soon as the numerical advantage at the back is restored there can be a switch to more aggressive defending to try and win the ball.

Coaching the Juventus 3-5-2: Defending

Compensating for a 3 v 3 Situation at the Back

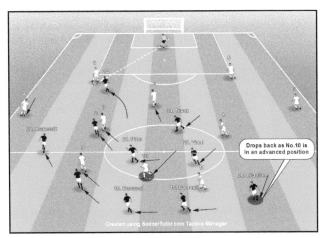

Finally in this example it is the No.10 who moves into an advanced position. None of the midfielders drop back to control him, as the responsibility of marking is passed to one of the defenders.

Lichtsteiner (26)is the player who will take care of creating a numerical advantage at the back.

The centre back (4) passes to the right back (2). The left wing back Asamoah (22) moves to close him down while Pogba (6) moves into a supporting position and Llorente (14) drops back to narrow the passing lane towards No.7.

Lichtsteiner (26) is in an effective position and there is already a 3 v 2 numerical advantage at the back, so Chiellini (3) can follow No.9's movement and mark him tightly.

Bonucci (19) shifts towards the strong side and takes over No.10's marking.

The right back (2) plays a long pass towards No.10. Bonucci (19) contests him aggressively as the tactical situation favours it.

These kinds of passes were usually very easy for the Juventus defenders who would win the ball or clear it from danger.

Coaching the Juventus 3-5-2: Defending

Starting Positions Before Pressing On the Right (Option 1)

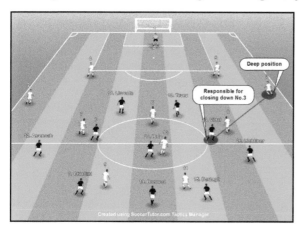

In situations when the pressing would take place on Juve's right side and the opposition's No.10 was in front of the deepest midfielder (Pirlo), both wing backs took up advanced positions.

Deciding which player put pressure on the left back (when he was in possession) depended on their positioning - whether they were deep or in an advanced position.

In the diagram we show the left back (3) in a deep position and Vidal (23) would be the player to apply pressure.

Starting Positions Before Pressing On the Right (Option 2)

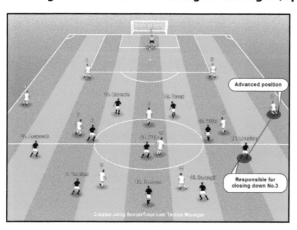

When the opposition's left back was in an advanced position, putting pressure on him as soon as he received the ball was the responsibility of the right wing back (Lichtsteiner).

Starting Positions Before Pressing On the Right (Option 3)

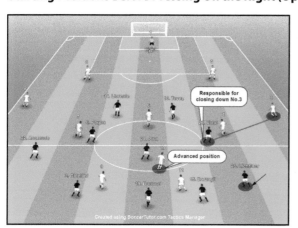

When the No.10 was in an advanced position behind the deepest midfielder (usually Pirlo), Lichtsteiner (26) would drop back to form a four man defence and make sure that Juventus retained a 4 v 3 numerical advantage at the back.

In this particular situation, Vidal (23) was responsible for putting pressure on the left back regardless of whether he was in a deep or advanced position.

Aggressive Marking of the Forward in Possession When Pressing On the Right

The pass from the goalkeeper is directed to the centre back (5). The white No.10 is in an advanced position high up the pitch and behind the Juventus midfield line.

The right wing back Lichtsteiner's (26) starting position is deep and as the ball travels towards No.5, he shifts slightly towards the right in order to stay close to the defenders and retain the numerical advantage at the back.

The other wing back Asamoah (22) does not have to drop too deep.

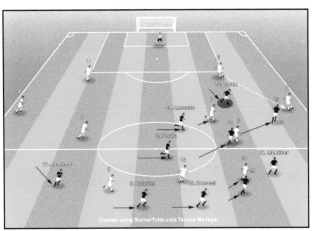

The centre back (5) passes to the left back (3). Vidal (23)moves to close him down and Tevez (10) drops back into a balanced position to control both the pass towards No.5 and the pass towards the defensive midfielder (6).

Pirlo (21) shifts as part of a chain reaction and takes over No.8's marking. The right wing back Lichtsteiner (26)remains close to the other defenders.

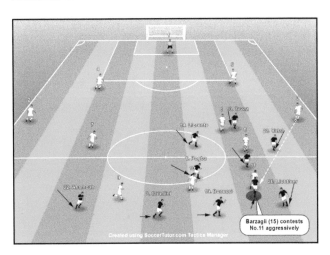

The left back (3) passes to No.11. Barzagli (15) moves forwards to aggressively contest the new man in possession with the aim of winning the ball immediately or forcing him to make a bad first touch.

Pirlo (21) moves back to help double mark No.11. Lichtsteiner (26) and Bonucci (19) move inwards from their positions to provide cover.

Barzagli (15) contests No.11 aggressively

Coaching the Juventus 3-5-2: Defending

CPSIA information can be obtained
at www.ICGtesting.com
Printed in the USA
BVHW021325280719
554316BV00010B/17/P